D0463541

Darrell Royal Talks Football

DARRELL

ROYAL

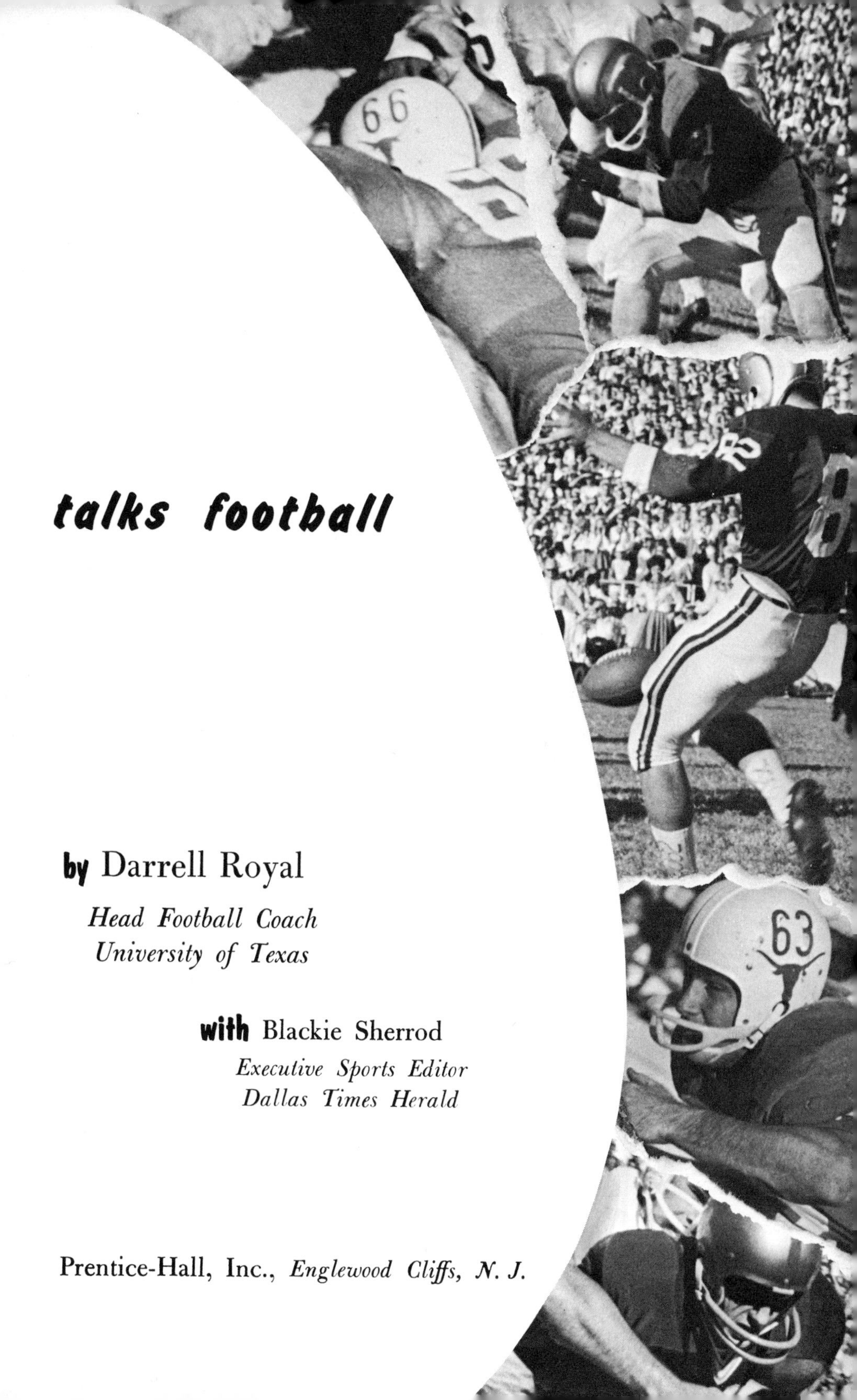

talks football

by Darrell Royal

Head Football Coach
University of Texas

with Blackie Sherrod

Executive Sports Editor
Dallas Times Herald

Prentice-Hall, Inc., *Englewood Cliffs, N. J.*

ALL RIGHTS RESERVED, INCLUDING THE RIGHT TO REPRODUCE THIS BOOK, OR ANY PORTIONS THEREOF, IN ANY FORM, EXCEPT FOR THE INCLUSION OF BRIEF QUOTATIONS IN A REVIEW.

Darrell Royal Talks Football, by Darrell Royal with Blackie Sherrod

© 1963 by Prentice-Hall, Inc., Englewood Cliffs, N. J.

Library of Congress Catalog Card Number: 63-16741

Third printing...... November, 1963

PRINTED IN THE UNITED STATES OF AMERICA

19684—BC

foreword

In the 1949 Sugar Bowl football game, we were worried about trying to contain North Carolina's excellent forward passing battery with Charles "Choo Choo" Justice throwing and Art Weiner, their fine 6-foot 4-inch end, receiving.

We decided to put Darrell Royal, our 5-foot 10-inch, 160-pound halfback, on Weiner. Comparing them physically, this seemed somewhat like a mismatch. Weiner was not only a skillful catcher and cutter, he stood half a foot taller and weighed 40 pounds more. But as so often happens in football, a physical contrast of two players does not tell the whole story. Royal had a fierce pride, great quickness and ability to react.

After Weiner caught one 22-yard pass early in the game, Royal began to stalk him relentlessly. Time after time, Justice threw to Weiner, running Carolina's most

A Word on Darrell Royal

By Bud Wilkinson

baffling patterns, but Royal, motivated by his sense of team pride, broke up pass after pass.

The climax came late in the first half when Justice led a Carolina march that reached from the Tar Heel 15-yard line to the Oklahoma 16. We led 7-6 at the time. From our 16, Justice passed to Weiner over the goal. Royal leaped high to flash in front of the ball and knock it down to save a touchdown. After completing a 7-yard pass to another Carolina receiver, Justice shot a final throw to Weiner. Closely guarded by Royal, Weiner could not get his hands on it. On the next play our line rushed Justice furiously as he faded, and Stan West and Ed Lisak tackled him before he could throw.

We were fortunate to score another touchdown in the last half and won, 14-6. Royal dogged Weiner all through the last half. With the exception of one 7-yard completion, the big Carolina end caught no more passes. Royal's determined defense was a tremendous factor in our victory.

Royal's ambition inspired him to perfect himself in so many different phases of the game that I believe he was among the most versatile backs I have ever seen. He hated to be mediocre at anything. He worked constantly to better himself in every related area of football.

He became the greatest spot punter I have ever coached. In that North Carolina game, he kicked all eight of his punts over the sideline or end line, giving Carolina no runbacks. He had punting power, too, booting one 81 yards against Oklahoma State. Against Missouri in 1947 he kicked out of bounds inside their 3-yard line on three successive kicks. They fumbled after the third one. We recovered to win the game.

He was an ace punt-returner as well, scoring against Kansas State with a 95-yard runback and against Kansas with one for 73 yards.

As a senior, we used him at quarterback for the first time and he handled the difficult position with complete poise and finesse. As a passer, he completed 20 of 37 for five touchdowns and had only two intercepted. A slashing ball-carrier, he scored 30 points on runs. He always set up the ball for our conversion booters. And going back to his pass defense, he set a career record of 17 interceptions that still stands at Oklahoma.

Darrell has put this same pride, this same delight and determination in doing his best, into his coaching. He wants every phase of it to be complete and concise. He strives to perfect every detail of his team's execution on defense, kicking, and attack just as he painstakingly perfected every aspect of football as a player at Oklahoma in 1946-1949.

The theme of Darrell's book is that pride is the basic element in winning football. I totally agree.

This is a fine football book in all respects. I commend it to you.

Table of Contents

List of Illustrations

Darrell Royal Talks Football

chapter one

In 1949, four seniors from the Oklahoma squad were invited to the Senior Bowl game in Jacksonville.

Jim Owens, Stan West, Wade Walker and I were the happy delegates from an Oklahoma squad that had just won 21 straight games.

It was just another all-star game. I couldn't tell you the score today, but I do know that we lost.

In the dressing room after the game, you could see the guys who had been associated with losing teams, laughing and joking and mapping out plans of attack for the night hours. One slapped Owens on the back and said, "Aw, forget about it, Jim, ole Bo is used to it, too." (Bo McMillin was our all-star coach.)

But the Oklahoma faces were so long we could have eaten oats out of a churn. We were bitter and dejected and

Pride and Winning Football

you could have bought the entire bunch for two bits, including tax. We had lost, and we just weren't used to it.

I've since coached in all-star games where our team lost and the boys who came off winning college squads were burned up about it. But the boys who played on teams that seldom won, why, they usually didn't give a plugged copper during the course of the game, much less afterward.

Pride Is the Basis of Winning Football

If I have any philosophy of this wonderful sport, it is this: Pride is what causes a winning team performance.

What's a fellow got to lose after he's had his pants dusted several times? It's just old shoe to him. When you

lose your pride (and defeats will drain it like a leech), then you just can't generate much firepower.

So that's what I consider the *primary* task of a head football coach. Plant, fertilize, groom and develop that pride. Some might think a head coach is chiefly concerned with drawing X's and O's on a blackboard, or teaching a halfback the double-clutching, E-flat, crossover sidestep. Nope!

The University of Texas football team would fare just as well if I didn't coach a lick. Our staff handles most of the instructing. I have confidence that Jim Pittman and Russell Coffee will herd the offensive linemen. Mike Campbell has been teaching the defensive ends and linebackers for several years. Charlie Shira is an old hand with the defensive guards and tackles. T. Jones' specialty is the defensive backs. Bob Schulze runs his freshmen squad. Bill Ellington and I work with the offensive backs, although I may concentrate on the quarterbacks. Fortunately we've been together long enough so that everyone thinks alike and it's automatically understood what we're looking for in the way of technical tutoring.

But a head coach is guided by this main objective: dig, claw, wheedle, coax that fanatical effort out of the players. You want them to play every Saturday as if they were planting the flag on Iwo Jima.

The Trademark of Greatness

This wild-eyed effort is a trademark of several college teams over the country: Arkansas teams; Louisiana State teams; Notre Dame teams have always been noted for their all-out pace.

Matty Bell, athletic director at Southern Methodist, once marvelled over Frank Broyles' teams at Arkansas. "I've always considered it a tough job to inspire a team to play fanatical football once or twice a season," said Matty, "but Broyles' teams play every game as if their lives were at stake."

A newspaperman once described a Texas team effort as:

> The **Longhorns** played like Rocky Marciano after somebody insulted his mother and was trying to push him off a raft into a river full of crocodiles.

I'd like to read that review every Sunday morning! That's the sort of trademark every coach wants.

Of course, there is nothing that develops pride like a winning tradition and a winning history.

Back when Oklahoma had its winning streak of 47 games going, a reporter asked Bud Wilkinson if there weren't an increasing strain on him and his squad, if the pressure weren't building up so that it was almost unbearable.

Bud said no, indeed, that a long winning streak was a welcome burden. It was an asset, not a liability. He loved that kind of pressure.

I vote for that. I'll even stuff the ballot box.

It's that old New York *Yankee* legend. You take an ordinary baseball player and stuff him into that pin-striped *Yankee* uniform and he automatically plays better than he can.

A weather-beaten old saying is that winning isn't everything, but it is way ahead of whatever comes in second. Coaches have always yelled it, painted it on locker room signs, and Rodgers and Hart have set it to music and any day now, they'll make a movie of it with Elvis Presley as the star halfback.

Pleasant Past

The University of Texas, quite fortunately, has had a winning history down through the years.

That winning history helps to get your team ready to play on Saturday. You, as coach, are able to tell the squad, "You're representing the best. Your reputation is established. When you put on this uniform, it's *expected* of you to go after the other man. You're *expected* to be aggressive and carry the fight. There's something wrong with you if you don't."

Back when Billy Cannon was grabbing off honors at Louisiana State, I heard an LSU coach say, "What makes Cannon a great player is his tremendous pride. When he runs out on the field and looks up at those 70,000 people, he thinks about just one thing. He's determined that every one of those spectators will leave the stadium after the game convinced they've seen the best halfback in the country."

Powerfully Positive Thinking

Most philosophers, I suppose, call it Positive Thinking. But I've always thought Positive Thinking, like luck, can run to two extremes. A neighbor once told me about her youngster who was to run in his grammar school's track meet the next day.

"Mom, those boys are bigger than I am and I think they're going to beat me," he said.

His mother corrected him. "Now that's not the right attitude, Tommy. You must think positively."

"Okay," he said sadly, "I'm *positive* they're gonna beat me!"

I'd much rather subscribe to the gospel of Leo Durocher, which was so typified in a story during the 1951 season. Bob Cooke, a sportscaster, interviewed Leo during the last week of the season.

"Barring the unforeseen, Leo, will your club win the pennant?"

"Whaddayuh mean by that?" roared Durocher. "There ain't gonna *be* no unforeseen!"

Rocky Marciano wasn't going to be pushed off that raft, either. Not while he was alive. That's why he was a winner.

A few years ago we went to play another college in an important game. In talking to the squad, I could put it to them bluntly: "If you go out there and get after them, they'll choke. Now they're a little bit better than we are, but they don't believe it because they've had their tails kicked too many times. Down deep inside, they don't believe they're as good as we are."

Now that's a cocky approach and it's rather delicate to be talking about: to say the other team is a choker. It would be disastrous if the other school knew that I had told our squad that. But it's the truth. When it gets right down to the wood-chopping, it is most important to have that deep confidence that your team is going to win and that you represent the best.

Winners' Group Is Exclusive

Now it's a simple matter of mathematics that all schools can't have winning traditions. I know. I've been on both sides of the fence. And I consider myself fortunate now to be associated with a school that does have that sort of background. It's been built up over many, many years under a number of coaches. And there is no substitute for it.

Certainly this background doesn't mean that you always will have a contending team. The cycle of good and bad seasons catches up to everyone sooner or later, just as sure as there's gravy on Chill Wills' vest. But that important instillation of pride, both individual and team, is much easier when your school has a winning history.

Frankly, coaches at high schools and colleges without that sort of history are at a marked disadvantage.

Now then. When your school has a winning background, you're going to be the foremost target for ambush. There's no question in my mind that everybody shoots for the University of Texas. Most big state universities are prime targets. Most opponents would rather beat us than any other team. But that's not a handicap. I just hope I'm never at a place where people are not aware we're in business.

The Bitter Pill of Defeat

In 1961, the Texas team was unbeaten through eight games and ranked No. 1 in those national polls that everyone seems to abide by. We were knocked off by Texas Christian and it was a bitter, bitter pill. That 0-6 game squashed a hope that the Southwest Conference would have its first national champion in 20 years, and it was a big story on sports pages across the country.

Still, I hope we can stay in a position where we make news when we lose, rather than when we upset somebody.

Players with Pride Are the Last to Surrender

You may remember the appraisal of Bobby Layne, by his old Detroit *Lion* teammate, Doak Walker:

"Bobby never lost a football game in his life," said Doak. "Time just ran out on him a few times."

Texas had a linebacker, a young firebrand named Pat Culpepper, with the same inner construction. If you were seven points behind and three minutes to go, some people would be ready to head for the barn and get that harness off. Not Culpepper. He figured the scoreboard would be changed pretty quick now. Maybe on the next play. He had too much pride to think of the situation any other way.

So—you must have pride to win consistently. And you must win consistently to establish a winning tradition that sustains pride. It all seems like an endless cycle.

Pride Is Where You Find It

All this is easy to say, but just how do you go about finding such boys, developing such pride?

Frankly, I don't know how you instill pride. Almost all football players have it when they begin competing.

Figure 1: An ingredient of the "bitter pill." TCU's fullback, Tommy Crutcher, rips off seven yards before *Longhorns* George Brucks (66) and Johnny Treadwell (60) bring him down. Texas had been ranked No. 1 nationally through eight wins of the 1961 season before losing to TCU.

Some lose it along the way, because they get discouraged at their own performances or at the team's fortunes.

Sometimes you'll find a lad who'll be a standout performer on a mediocre team, a battler who'll keep sticking his helmet in the tough spots even though his team is taking a beating. Here is a boy with rare pride because he's having to play solo. He doesn't have the contagious pride of teammates to add fuel to his flame. This is the high school prospect all colleges are seeking.

There are certain prep school areas in the country that breed football pride. Places like Massillon, Ohio, and other high school hotbeds in Northern Ohio. And spots like Abilene and Odessa and Breckenridge in West Texas, where youngsters have a burning desire to play high school football from the time they are able to tell a ball from a pumpkin. This is a contagious sort of pride that keeps the teams winning.

Now—whether winning begets pride, or pride begets winning, in those high school hotbeds, no one can say. It's the old chicken-and-egg proposition. But one is necessary to the other.

Other Factors Sustaining Pride

Once a college has recruited high school players with pride (or a squad nucleus), then the feeling may be maintained and developed by several methods: (1) By offering a first class athletic program with top drawer accommodations. (2) By installing the young men in first-class housing, feeding them first-class food, helping them to establish a sound set of values that apply to the classroom as well as to athletic fields. (3) By keeping the athletes in school until graduation, so you'll have older, more mature squad members to provide leadership.

Sometimes you'll find a lad whose pride has been injured along the way and he won't be real sure of himself. Suddenly he'll look around his first-class dormitory room, and his clean, well-stocked dining room and he'll see the confidence and assurance of his teammates and it'll grab hold of him like the red measles.

And these are the young men who carry the fight across No Man's Land and deposit it in the enemy lap.

Sic 'Em Football

Have you ever owned a dog that was just a bit uncertain?

When you whistled at him, he didn't know whether to "sic 'em" or "come here"?

Well, the boy who knows you mean "sic 'em," that's the young man all coaches are looking for. There's no doubt in his mind. He sics 'em, because that's the only way to win and because he's too proud to lose.

That's what a coach must sell to his young charges. The basic formula of winning football is so elemental. You can cloak it under fancy names, sew ruffles on it, run it up the flagpole, but it's just as simple as a screwdriver. If football teams are anywhere near being in the same category, it's the team with pride that rakes in the chips.

chapter two

Occasionally during a football season, a coach wrestles with insomnia. Instead of counting sheep jumping over a fence, he sees left halfbacks dropping screen passes and centers bouncing the ball to the punter. I have found a personal cure for sleeplessness, if it could only be arranged at the proper time and place.

At a football clinic or a gathering of coaches, let somebody get up to the blackboard, start drawing play diagrams and lecturing on the complexities of the junction block by the fullback or similar subjects, and I can work up a snore with remarkable ease.

There have been some great football coaches who dwelt on technical thoroughness. Dr. Jock Sutherland, the famous Pittsburgh coach, once lectured two solid hours on a single off-tackle play. I certainly don't wish to criticize

The Simple Life in Coaching

devoted attention to detail. We have all learned from these technicians. The plays the offenses are running, the blocking assignments, the defensive moves . . . they are essential and your coaching staff must know them well and teach them thoroughly.

The Why's of Football

But the really interesting information, I think, is what the other coaches are doing in regard to squad discipline, squad morale, squad aggressiveness and similar aspects of the business.

When a coach starts talking about why he did a certain thing, why he installed a certain play, that's when I perk up and start listening. Not how he did it, but why.

People often ask about the shop talk when coaches get together—say, when Bobby Dodd, Frank Broyles, Woody Hayes, and some of us gather in a hotel room for a bull session.

Well, for one thing, we very seldom draw diagrams.

What I usually ask is, when they stop their scrimmaging during the week, how much hard work do they schedule or how they can tell when to lighten their drills? I'm always interested when they talk about the psychological approach to their squads. What is their relationship with the players? Is it stern? Is it informal? I want to know how they handle a squad before a game. Do they favor a long warm-up drill or would they rather stay longer in the dressing room? I'm interested in how their coaching authority is delegated, what is the chain of command in the athletic department, how they work with their publicity directors, even how they plan and fill their television programs.

As an example, the question most frequently asked me nowadays is about the Flip-Flop Offense, which was originated at Texas in 1961. Coaches want to know the reasoning behind it, why we switch our linemen from one side to the other, how it has been to our advantage. They don't care about the selection of personnel or what plays we're running. They can diagram most blocking assignments on most everyone's plays in deepest sleep. They want to know why we felt this offensive plan was an advantage.

The Coaching Brotherhood

Contrary to public belief, most college coaches get along well together. There may be a few enemies, but not many. Of course, a coach may be more competitive toward some teams than others. In my case, most of the time the coaches are my best friends even though our schools may be deadly rivals.

You may think your wife and your teen-age daughters are telephone nuts, but you should see a head coach's phone bill. Coaches are constantly visiting over the phone, especially during the season. Sometimes they trade ideas on different techniques or ask opinions on upcoming opponents. Or sometimes they just want to talk, to spread their nervousness and misery around. I remember once, right before the Texas-Rice game in 1958, I called Bobby Dodd at Atlanta. Texas was undefeated through five games and we had beaten Oklahoma for the first time in six years and some of our backers had homesteaded on Cloud Nine.

I felt we were overrated and that the team wasn't enthusiastic enough. There was a hornet's nest waiting for us in Houston and we were walking into it like Little Red Riding Hood with jam on her face.

I didn't especially want any advice from Coach Dodd; mainly, I suppose, it was a plea for sympathy. I described the squad symptoms, the apparent attitude. He'd been down that same road several times in the past, but he couldn't help. He laughed and said it sounded as if we were in bad trouble. He was so accurate: something like 34-7.

Coaches' Approaches

Some of the more dedicated "students of the game" have put on their deep-thinking caps and classified different "psychological schools" of coaching—the different approaches used by various coaches to communicate with their squads.

Of course, there was the bombastic, dramatic personality of Knute Rockne, who played on young emotions so successfully. Another Notre Dame coach, Frank Leahy, was famous for oratorical splendor that seemed to inspire his squads.

Coach Bryant, in his three stops at Kentucky, Texas A&M and Alabama, is always in the conversation with his coaching technique, which is usually called the Bear Bryant "Hard-Nose School." And many are the stories thereof.

His 1957 Texas *Aggies* were playing Arkansas in the Ozark hills and Bryant's team, with the great John David Crow, was unbeaten through six games.

The *Aggies* had a 7-6 lead late in the game when A&M quarterback Roddy Osborne, for some strange reason, called a flat zone pass. Arkansas halfback Donnie Stone picked off the pass and lit a shuck down the sideline. It looked like a certain *Razorback* touchdown and, consequently, a *Razorback* victory and maybe a Bear Bryant fit of apoplexy.

But here came Osborne, angling across the field as if Lucifer himself were in the rumble seat. Somehow he caught Stone after a long chase, and the touchdown was staved off. The *Aggies* preserved their one-point margin and their 13th straight win.

After the game, a dressing room visitor asked Osborne, "Was there any doubt in your mind that you could catch Stone?"

"No," said Osborne, glancing at the stern-faced Bryant and shuddering. "Stone was running for a touchdown, but I was running for my *life!*"

Old Bear rumbles around and says, "Aw, there ain't nothing to this fancy football. I'd druther just throw 22 men out on the field and see who can outbutt the othern."

This may be the popular image of Bryant, but let me assure you he doesn't have horns sprouting out of his forehead, nor does he tote around a cat-o'-nine-tails, and he is certainly one of the most astute and meticulous defensive technicians in the business today.

The Other "Schools"

You've heard about the Stern Fundamentalism of Bowden Wyatt and other Tennessee exes; the Charm School of Bud Wilkinson at Oklahoma and Paul Dietzel at Army; the Soft Sell of Bobby Dodd at Georgia Tech; the Spittin' and Whittlin' philosophy of Frank Howard at Clemson and Abe Martin at TCU; the Loosey-Goosey Relaxation of Duffy Daugherty, etc.

That's the way these various portraits have been painted, anyway, and I suppose it's fairly accurate. It makes pretty good newspaper reading for all the fans anyway.

But all these coaches, whether on the South Forty or Fifth Avenue, in overalls or a silk suit, are attempting to accomplish the same purpose: get their people to intimidate the other side.

And the foremost rule of any psychological approach is Be Natural.

You can't copy any of these coaches. A coach must be himself. I couldn't be a Bear Bryant. I wouldn't last a year. I don't think I could be a Bud Wilkinson, although I played under him and have been greatly influenced by him. I have to be a Royal, for better or for worse.

If you're not completely natural, you couldn't convince your players that Doris Day is a girl.

The New, Sophisticated Player

The collegiate player of today has no more basic intelligence than the oldtimer, of course. The current athlete does have better training, better equipment, more coaching, earlier coaching, more opportunities. And the present species exists in greater numbers. No, they're no more intelligent, but they seem more "worldly" now, if that is the word.

The players have broader concepts, more diversified interests. And it's a mistake to treat them with sandpile rules.

When I was a youngster, it was a red-letter event to get 100 miles away from Hollis, Oklahoma. Nowadays, half your squad may have danced on the *Starlight Roof,* toured Canada on a bicycle or had an audience with the Pope.

It is a smaller world, all the way round.

In all probability, youngsters are harder for a coach to fool nowadays. (If a coach is foolish enough to think he can fool them.) Perhaps it's more correct to say a coach can't *sway* a team as once he could.

In other words, I couldn't go before the Texas squad and give them a good old blood-and-guts pep talk such as Rockne used to inspire Notre Dame players. Today's kids are too smart for that. I couldn't rant and rave through an emotional spiel; they would see right through me and start measuring me for a paper hat.

When the Tension Mounts

That's not to say that I never get emotional over a ball game. Any coach does. I get fired up and the players can sense when that happens and I think it has a tendency to make them join me.

Dutch Meyer, who held forth many years at TCU, thinks the psychological approach by coaches has undergone more change than any other phase of the game in the past four decades. He thinks psychology still plays a major part in game preparation, but it is much more subtle than it was in the old days.

"When Matty Bell was coaching the TCU varsity," Dutch said, "and I was coaching the freshmen, we didn't think we were doing a good job unless we had 'em crying when they left the dressing room.

"I changed my mind about that," said Dutch. "I learned my big lesson in the 1935 game with SMU."

That game still is a Southwestern classic. SMU, with its great stars Harry Shuford and Bobby Wilson, and TCU, with Sammy Baugh, were both unbeaten and untied when they met in their annual rivalry. A *Rose Bowl* bid awaited the winner.

"I had the best receivers in college football—as good as any receivers, anytime," said Dutch. "Yet I gigged 'em up so high that they went out and dropped nine of Sammy Baugh's passes. I had them too excited.

"But it used to be that we gigged 'em up as high as we could. We put on that oratory and had them tight as a fiddle string—ready to tear the other team apart.

"That stuff won't work now. A modern football player can't do all the things he has to do—can't remember them—if he is gigged up. He has to be relaxed. He has to think.

They do things in football now like angle blocking and diagonal stuff that we didn't know about."

Trick Psychology Does Not Work Today

Certainly it is out of the question today for a coach to try to hoodwink a team, or to use trick psychology. As much time as a coach spends with his squad, as much as he's in front of them, talking, he'd be silly to think he could deceive them in any way.

If I feel something strongly enough, I'll say it, and it might be emotional or even on the rah-rah side. I don't see anything wrong with climbing on the soapbox and waving the flag if you're sincere about it. If it is an honest feeling, I think it is accepted by the squad. But phoney business is not appreciated by the present generation, and they'll laugh you out of the hall.

Neither do I mean to say that Rockne's furious speeches were a gimmick or trick psychology. I'm positive it was completely natural with him, just as it would be *unnatural* to other coaches. Some people are just constructed that way. You know people whom you can listen to and get tense and on edge because they're so crammed with enthusiasm. I know coaches like that.

Youthful Enthusiasm and Interest

I don't believe today's players, for all their worldliness, are any harder to stir up emotionally.

They're probably even more emotional than they used to be, but they work up this fervor among themselves. It is generated quietly without any sort of wild-eyed encouragement.

One reason why performances are better today is the vastly increased interest in football. There is wider coverage by television, broader reporting by the newspapers. There are more people in the stadiums and more prestige to the winners, more national honors and recognition.

And every Saturday, we should be more thankful to some forgotten Princeton student, who fortunately lost his aplomb at the 1869 Princeton-Rutgers game.

The two teams were shoving each other around with primitive vigor when one of the Princetonians leaped in the air and yelled, "Siss, boom, ah."

It wasn't quite clear what his motive was, at first. Perhaps several of his neighbors suspected he had sat down on a lighted cigar. But other Princetonians remembered the yell and joined in. Soon they had a thing going.

That "siss, boom, etc.' happened to be the favorite outcry of the Seventh Regiment of New York.

The Seventh Regiment was a Union outfit that once passed through the Princeton campus on its way south to meet Johnny Reb. The soldiers had a sort of "rocket yell" to pass away the time. The students heard this yell and admired it greatly. They kept it for their very own, but they probably had scant occasion to use it, save when they happened to sit on a lighted cigar or when they had to do a rocket imitation in dormitory charades.

But it was just perfect for football. And when this Princeton student suddenly remembered it and gave vocal vent, it was quickly adopted and cultivated into the first collegiate cheer.

The finished product went something like: "Rah, rah, rah . . . tiger, tiger, tiger . . . siss, siss, siss . . . boom, boom, boom . . . aaaaahhhhhhhHHH. . . Princeton! Princeton! Princeton!"

Within a few years all this was organized. The fellows yelled in unison and had a high old time doing it. Some of the more Union-minded chaps jumped out in front of the crowd and waved their hands about. They were the first cheerleaders.

Several of us may sometimes forget just how important are those cheers and the accompanying enthusiasm.

Now if you want to see an emotionless game, you take

away that band and the twirlers and the cheering sections. You take away that newspaper coverage and the television and radio. Take away the crowds and put two teams together on a vacant lot and tell them to have at it. You'll see the darndest mess of pushing and pulling and a complete absence of people pursuing and whacking each other. It would be duller than an amateur wrestling match between King Farouk and Elsa Maxwell.

It's the fanfare and the whoopla and the batons and drums and headlines that prompt these real go-gettum efforts.

Keep It Simple

Once upon a time, as the story always goes, there was an old sea captain who was greatly respected as a wise, although reserved, skipper. He commanded vessels for 50 years and he had a peculiar habit that kept his officers and crew perpetually curious.

Each morning, right after mess, he would return to his cabin, open a safe in the bulkhead, remove a slip of paper and study it carefully. He would return the paper to the safe and go about his business of being a sage, respected old sea dog.

Finally the captain died at sea and his staff could hardly restrain themselves. The first mate rushed to the captain's cabin and found the wallsafe open. He took out the slip of paper and read it carefully:

"Port—left. Starboard—right."

All of which is a roundabout way of illustrating another firm conviction: football is growing entirely too complicated for its own good.

Avoid Mistakes

There is the alarming tendency to stray away from the old basics of blocking, tackling, kicking, and avoiding mistakes. These are the flour and salt and meal of football, and if you try to mix them with a lot of other fancy ingredients, you may miss out on your daily bread.

If there is anything a winning football team must do, it is to treat mistakes like a copperhead in the bedclothes. Avoid them with all the energy you can muster.

I firmly believe this: As a coach, you may be a real high-domer. You may have a doctorate from M.I.T. and be way ahead of other coaches in what you're trying to instruct your team to do. You may be smarter than, say, all the rest of the coaches in football. You can invent something new, imaginative, another dimension in football that's frightening in its potential. But if you can't get these ideas completely across to your squad—even though it's a great system of theories—then you have about as much chance as a stump-tailed bull in flytime. Old Joe McDoakes, chewing tobacco, teaching the short punt formation and playing a seven-diamond defense, will throw a fire-eating team at you and knock your innovation out of the ball park.

A Confused Player Cannot Be Aggressive

If a player is the least bit confused, he can't be aggressive. Tattoo that on your wall. Or better still, on your wallet. You *must* play aggressive football to win, and you cannot be aggressive and confused at the same time.

You may think a player is not giving his best effort. I've looked at game movies and thought: that Jones kid is dogging it. He couldn't play first jumper on the Vassar quoits team. And later I've found out that the Jones kid was simply confused. Let him get everything straight in his mind and be sure of his movements and purpose, and he'll move mountains for you.

A coach should do anything in his power to eliminate confusion and create good morale. You can't have good morale with confused boys huddled together like sheep before a north wind.

Example: Many squads use a varied starting count by

Figure 2: A well-executed play. The signal is given by Texas' Mike Cotten and the line eagerly starts forward, getting the jump on the TCU defense. The automatic reaction of the entire offense is obvious as the play begins explosively.

the quarterback. They'll break the rhythm of the snap signal. The quarterback may bark, "*Hut-two, hut-two,* (pause) *hut-two,*" and then the ball is snapped. Certainly it might keep the defense wary and uncertain of when to charge. But it also handicaps the charge by your own offensive linemen.

If your linemen have to strain and listen to tell exactly when they're going to take that first step, then they can't be concentrating on those individual guys on the other side of the line of scrimmage. We've tried it, as almost every team has. But we've found our linemen are having to think too much about *when* they can charge. They can't devote their wholehearted attention to beating the fellow facing them.

After the ball is snapped, football is simply a process of reaction. A player doesn't have time to think, "Well, let's see, I gotta step off on my right foot and if he moves this way, I gotta use my right flipper instead of my left flipper. Or maybe I'll sag and give a little ground on defense, or submarine and meet the flood of blockers."

This boy doesn't have time to think. He must have an automatic reaction to all situations. He must move like the village oaf who happened by the blacksmith shop one day. The smithy was hard at his business, hammering out a white-hot horseshoe. The bumpkin asked what it was, and the smithy told him it was a horseshoe and invited him to take a look.

The poor fellow picked up the blistering shoe and quickly dropped it while the blacksmith roared with laughter.

"What's the matter?" the smithy said.

"Nothing," said the bumpkin, wringing his hand. "It just don't take me all day to look at a horseshoe."

Be Quick or Dead

It would be pleasant and convenient if a player had all day to look at his horseshoe; to decide how wide he should play, or how tight, or what sort of a charge would be best in this certain situation. But football is a game of quickness and a certain amount of hectic confusion is unavoidable. From a vantage point high in the stands, the game looks clearly defined, the plays are outlined sharply, and the action is slowed down by the actual eyeball distance from the scene.

But down on the field, it is a massive, jumbled traffic jam of young bodies, lunging and grunting and straining without the advantage of perspective.

A player must be trained thoroughly, he must repeat the same drills over and over in practice, so that he automatically responds to a situation. If his mind is cluttered up by a lot of decisions, he won't react properly. He'll freeze.

Progress Toward Simplicity

At Texas, we made more progress in simplification when the Flip-Flop offense was installed than we really expected. We'll go into the Flip-Flop details later, but basically it is a plan of using strongside and weakside linemen, so that the same lineman will always play the same relative position according to the balance of the formation. He'll have the same blocking assignment whether he's stationed on the right or left side of center.

This cut our blocking assignments at least in half. We had only one guard who pulled out of line to run interference. He was the same guard every time, although he might be on the left side of center one play, and the right side on the next play. You can readily see that this trimmed our guards' assignments to learn.

Our linemen, under the Flip-Flop plan, have only five plays where they block at the point of attack. In other words, they have just five blocking assignments to learn.

This doesn't count downfield blocking, but that phase of football isn't complicated. Downfield blocking is just a matter of effort and hustle. The only time a lineman really has to think is when the play is directed right over him.

When Variety Is Not the Spice of Life

Many coaches still have a multitude of plays. There are more coaches who have *too many plays* than coaches who don't have enough. I just don't know of any examples of coaches not having enough plays.

Take the Tennessee clan of coaches, disciples of Gen. Robert Neyland. Most of the time, Neyland never used more than 25 plays. He often testified that he never ran a play in a game before it had been rehearsed at least *500 times* in practice.

"It's not the number of plays you have," the general preached; "it's the way you execute them."

"You always knew what Neyland was going to do," said Alabama's Hank Crisp, "but just try to stop him."

Even today, Tennessee players of 20 years ago can come back to a reunion and they can sit down and talk intelligently about the offense the *Vols* are running right now. The coaching staff has stuck with the same single-wing offense year after year, and knows what it is looking for. By the time a boy becomes a senior, he knows exactly what the coaching staff is looking for.

In our own case, before the Flip-Flop, we were changing our Texas offense from week to week. We'd put in a set of plays for Baylor one week, then throw them out and put in another set for TCU the next week.

We did so much play changing and switching of blocking assignments when we began spring practice that it was all a jumbled mess. We actually had to start all over again. We had no carry-over value. This was before the Flip-Flop simplified everything and gave us a simple set of plays we stuck to, regardless of opponent.

However, this point must be repeated again and again. You don't win games with the Flip-Flop offense. You don't win with the Split T or the Winged T or the Unbalanced Goose-Step or the Man-in-Motion Thingamajig. You win games with aggressiveness and precise play execution, regardless of your offensive and defensive systems.

You must *force* things to happen: *make* the other team fumble; *push* their finger on the panic button; and *grab* the initiative.

And you must eliminate confusion to have this aggressiveness. Simplicity! It's wonderful.

chapter three

Then vs. Now

The quickest way to start an argument, other than telling the missus that lawn-mowing is good for her figure, is to compare the present-day athlete with the oldtimer. Pit the Mantles against the Ruths, the Listons against the Dempseys, the Palmers against the Joneses. Wars have been fought over less.

I was involved in such a tiff a few years back, the first season I was at Texas. We had a 6-3-1 record in 1957 and were invited to the Sugar Bowl, where Mississippi scorched us beyond recognition. It was a five-touchdown licking and, naturally, I wasn't exactly the Queen of the May in the dressing room afterward.

A writer asked how I thought our Mississippi conquerors compared to the unbeaten Oklahoma teams I had known as a player. I answered that this Mississippi team could have beaten the Sooners of my day. Then I added that this Texas team, although a 7-39 victim, also could have beaten those Oklahoma teams.

Well, sir, I might as well have called Will Rogers a horse thief. Oklahoma people, after reading that interview, set new high jump records all over the state. They climbed on my back with raking spurs for "low-rating" their Oklahoma heroes of the past.

Players Are Better Developed Today

Of course, I didn't mean it that way at all. I simply meant that football had progressed tremendously since the late 1940's. I also thought the Oklahoma team of 1957, and

several other teams of that year, could have beaten the Oklahoma teams of the 1940's, and perhaps I should have said that. I was trying to stress that *all* teams were improved, players were universally better, just as the high jumpers, the sprinters, the golfers are better than they were in the past.

Certainly there have been some physical changes over the last quarter-century. Players are larger. Remember, if you will, that the biggest member of the famous Four Horsemen of the 1924 Notre Dame team weighed about 167 pounds. To rate a glance today, a college back that size would have to be a gold-plated whiz and the son of the richest living alumnus.

Who's to say the sky is the limit? Look at Wilt Chamberlain. The sky comes up only to his shoulders on a clear day. Yet the day may be coming when Wilt Chamberlain will be an average height pro basketball player.

Red Auerbach, the gentleman in charge of the Boston *Celtics*, once said, "When I started coaching in 1946 with Washington, the average height of the National Basketball Association player was 6-1½. Today, pro players average around 6-6."

The Trend Is Upward

And it's not only athletes, you know. We're all going up through the roof. You're taller than your father, aren't you? Probably bigger around, too.

In 1900, less than four percent of American men were six feet tall. Nowadays, one out of every five is that height. Back in 1877, someone with an eye for the future put the tape measure to a group of 14-year-old boys in Boston. They measured 4-7½ and averaged 87 pounds. Today the average 14-year-old is eight inches taller and weighs 31 more pounds.

The first Miss America, Margaret Gorman, who won the title in 1921, stood only 5-1. The current queens stretch up to 5-7. Thirty years ago, the average man's suit size was size 38. Now, it is 42. New hotels order 80-inch beds instead of the old standard 74. Even bath towels are eight inches longer than they were, because you have more surface to swab off.

Better nutrition is part of the answer. Better control of childhood diseases and better health conditions. Also, scientists believe there is some sort of evolutionary force that has stimulated growth.

Goodness knows what this will make Wilt Chamberlain III, when he gets here, except an extremely highly paid basketball player and a menace to low-flying aircraft.

Growing Emphasis on Pursuit

What is the biggest change in the way football is played? I believe it is the over-all effort, the constant PURSUIT practiced by winning teams today.

"Pursuit" is possibly the most popular technical term in today's football nomenclature. Bowden Wyatt of Tennessee defines pursuit as "taking the shortest course to the ball carrier and arriving in a bad humor."

Abe Martin, the drawling boss at TCU, says, "I don't know about this pursuit business. We used to call it *chase 'em*."

Pursuit is simply an all-out effort on defense, a grim sprint on a collision course with the ball carrier, wherever he may be. To have pursuit, each forward defender must first protect his territory and then move to the ball. The course he takes is at an angle which will put him in front of the ball carrier at the earliest possible moment. It is important that he take the proper angle, else he may wind up at the depot after the train has left.

Today there is tremendous stress on fanatical effort being expended on each play. Especially is this noticeable on defense.

Evaluating Pursuit

Some coaches, in studying their game films, will stop the reel when a tackle is made and study the picture. Coach

Wilkinson holds that a team has good pursuit, or effort, if nine defenders are within eight yards of the ball carrier when the whistle is blown. If defenders are scattered out over the field, they're either confused, tired or just not trying to get acquainted with the enemy.

Charles McClendon, the LSU coach, uses a new twist in grading defensive play on the films. He gives credit only to the player who *first* makes contact with the ball carrier; he doesn't give credit for an *assist* on a tackle. This is Mac's way of emphasizing pursuit, getting there first, beating your teammates to the tackle.

We don't study or grade pursuit that closely at Texas. It's easy to tell if you're getting an outstanding defensive effort. It will look as if it's raining tacklers around the ball carrier.

That's the big reason you don't have 60-minute players on today's college fields. It is almost a physical impossibility for a young man to give maximum effort and perform at maximum efficiency on each play of a game.

Toughness of the Old Guard

I know there are all sorts of legends about the hardiness of the oldtime athletes . . . how they'd ride hot, dusty day coaches to a game site, eat a hot dog and play on a rock pile with copies of *College Humor* taped to their legs for shin guards.

Red Grange likes to tell about the toughness of his former Chicago *Bear* teammate, Bulldog Turner:

> Turner and I were roommates on road trips and one of our favorite pastimes was looking out our hotel window at the scenery below. Especially the feminine scenery. (This is one phase of football that will **never** change.) One afternoon Turner was inspecting the pretty sights from a fourth floor room, leaned out too far, and fell heavily to the sidewalk below. He hit flat on his back, making a rather

Figure 3: Here is Pursuit personified, and Texas quarterback Mike Cotten can testify to its effectiveness. Three TCU tacklers plow Cotten under, even though the first tackler missed his mark.

loud thwack, and creating a bit of confusion among the passing traffic. A policeman rushed over to Turner, who was calmly dusting off his clothes.

"What's the commotion here?" he demanded.

"Darned if I know, officer," said Bulldog. "I just got here myself."

Certainly the oldtimers were hardy. They had to be. They didn't have the equipment or the playing conditions available today.

All-out Play Is Sporadic

And they'll argue stoutly that they played just as hard in the old days as boys do now. But they didn't.

On defense, if the play headed in the other direction, they were more inclined to take it easy and not shift into high gear to get over where the action was. I know this will bring furious opposition from the Old School, but it is against the laws of human strength and endurance to exert 100 percent effort and 100 percent efficiency on 140 plays in a single afternoon.

There is no way that a player of today or yesteryear could come down here in this Texas heat, for example, and play 60 minutes the way we play. I'm talking about running at full speed on every punt, every kickoff, covering every pass, pursuing on every defensive play, making an initial block, then rising and heading downfield for another shot on every offensive play.

Modern Use of Movies

What has brought about this biggest change in college football, this dedicated pursuit?

Film study, for one thing.

The concentrated study of game movies has made coaches and players more conscious of all-out effort and aggressiveness on *every* play. A player's moves on every step of every play are a matter of celluloid record. He realizes this fact.

If he's a proud lad, he doesn't want his coaches studying the game film and seeing him loaf on any play. Subconsciously, perhaps, he wants to go on record as a bearcat.

Also, his job may depend upon these movies. If he's a first-stringer, he just might be demoted next week if the game films show some holding back on his part. If he's a second-stringer, his role in the film could advance him to a starting job.

At Texas, we'll spend around $11,000 a year on football films. We use two photographers on game movies, one with a wide-angle lens to cover the entire field, and one with a close-up lens to focus on the play itself. After a game these films are run and re-run by the coaching staff.

On any Monday in autumn, you can visit the Texas film room and see two offensive coaches seated at a "hand viewer," making notes on the previous game. A few feet away, a couple of defensive coaches will be using another hand viewer, whipping the film back and forth; one calling off plays while the other jots them down on a chart. Still another coach may be seated at his desk with a mirrored desk screen, running off a game film of the next opponent. Of course, we may all be in the market for seeing-eye dogs before many more years, but while the eyes last, they'll be fighting flickers.

Our game films are clipped and separated into three reels—the offensive plays, the defensive plays, the kicking plays.

The offensive coaches will pore over each play, searching for reasons why the play did or did not succeed. Each play is copied off on a game chart, telling down-and-distance, signal called, opposing defensive alignment, and play result.

Defensive coaches do the same. When the squad sees the game movie (on Monday night following the Saturday game), the players do not see the game in proper sequence. The offensive coaches will show the offensive reel to the players, pointing out mistakes and successes. Then the defensive coaches will show their reel to the squad. All the kicking plays—kickoffs, kickoff returns, punts, punt returns, field goals, conversions—are contained on another reel. It is usually shown on Wednesday or Thursday.

We use considerable film in practice. It is especially useful during the two-a-day workouts that precede the opening of school each September.

Improving a Specific Play or Player

Let's say, for example, we're having trouble with the option play. We'll set up a drill during the morning workout and film it from all angles.

By the time the morning workout is over, we shower, have lunch and return to the athletic offices, the film has been processed and is there waiting for us. Then we are able to contact the boys involved in the play, have them report to the stadium early that afternoon and show them the film before the late workout, so we can make corrections.

If we want to prove a point to the linebackers, we'll set the camera on a tower behind the defense and focus squarely on the linebacker's shoulder blades. This way we can tell if he is meeting the blockers head-on, or if he's running around a blocker and creating a gap.

There is absolutely nothing to compare with a boy seeing himself in action. You can stand and talk to him until your tongue wears out. You can tell him something 200 times and he may still doubt you. But he can see it on film and you only have to tell him once.

Take the common case of a blocker "position stepping." When a blocker is trying to move a defender to one side or the other, he'll take his first step for position and then make his attack. This is a common fault and it's hard to convince a boy that when he steps for position, his man may shoot right through his parking space and penetrate before the blocker ever makes contact. But you tell him and tell him and tell him and he'll look at you as if he just got off the boat from China. But take a film of him doing a simple one-on-one blocking drill and show it to him.

"Why, I'm position stepping!" he'll say. "Why didn't you say so?"

It is always rather embarrassing immediately after a game when newspapermen come into the dressing room and ask about this play, or what happened on that play, or who was the outstanding blocker or defender. There's no way I can answer those questions fairly and intelligently until after I see the films. Oh, on some occasions there is a standout play which is unreeled right out in the open and which may materially affect the outcome. But usually, the secrets are locked in those close quarters that are not always visible from the sidelines.

After studying the film, I can sit down with the writers and tell them who played well and how the game was won or lost. For that reason, I have a press conference each Monday noon with local writers, an occasional visiting writer and the wire service reporters, and I am able to give them a fairly comprehensible diagnosis of the game. By that time I have seen the films several times, listened to reports of the individual coaches and had a chance to determine the "why" of the previous Saturday.

Use of the Polaroid

There are other uses of films. Some coaches have rigged up a Polaroid camera with a long lens. A photographer, working from the pressbox, will snap pictures of a defensive alignment used by the opposition. The picture is printed in 10 seconds by whatever magic those cameras use, and a runner will hustle the print down to the bench where the coaches and the quarterbacks can study it.

There very probably is some merit to this practice. However, we feel we get the same information in quicker fashion from our assistant coaches in the pressbox, with a phone to the bench. It might be better to have the information in pictorial form, but it seems a little too elaborate for our uses.

Closed Circuit Television

There are coaches who have experimented with using closed circuit television during a game. Warren Giese used one of these contraptions when he brought his South Carolina team to Austin to play us. The television receiver was housed in a small tent by the bench, to keep out the light and make viewing clearer. We tried it out the following spring during an intra-squad game. Jim Pittman, one of our assistant coaches, could find only one use for the arrangement. If your team was taking a severe thumping, the coach would crawl in that tent and hide from the fans.

We couldn't use it successfully. Personally, I couldn't watch the television screen in the tent and get the feel of the game. I want to know just where the ball is, the down and distance, how the wind is blowing and a lot of things I just can't learn from a television screen.

Perhaps some day television will be perfected and used universally. I have heard about the possibility some day of a television taping arrangement so that films of the first half could be shown to the squad during the halftime intermission. At the present time, however, this would call for the purchase of a video-tape machine and it would be rather expensive for use only five times a year. There is some experimentation on quickly-developed film, one that takes only a minute to develop and print and project while it is still wet. When and if this process is perfected, it might be the answer to further aid from the cameras.

Population Explosion in Coaching Ranks

In addition to football films, another principal reason for development of pursuit is the increasing number of coaches.

There once were seven or eight outstanding coaches

in the nation. Now there are hundreds of top-notch football coaches just in the state of Texas. Where a head coach once worked with a two-man staff (and that wasn't so long ago), now he usually has eight or nine assistants. Georgia Tech, for example, often has 14 men on its football staff.

There are more colleges, turning out more coaches, who are better versed in technical football. There are more clinics, more literature, more communication between coaches.

Therefore, with more coaches, the players are more closely supervised, given more individual attention, graded and evaluated more minutely. A player is watched every second of practice and of game action. Hence, he is doubly impressed with the need for all-out effort on every play.

Better Conditioning: Outgrowth of Pursuit

Another change in today's football is a by-product of the increased tempo and aggressiveness of play. A player must keep himself in better physical condition than ever before.

The game is speeding up each year. It is more demanding of an all-out effort and the headlong participation of all eleven men on every play. There is more emphasis on kick coverage, pass coverage, never-halting hustle.

Perhaps you can remember when the first days of September football practice were almost a total waste. Players would be sore and bruised and limping around at half-speed until they got in shape. Nowadays, players should report in good physical condition. They must be ready for immediate all-out effort. Most coaches now have contact work in the first drill. If we have to take time to devote to conditioning players, we're in trouble.

Thus, it is up to the players themselves. Those two-a-day workouts at the start of fall are punishing. A boy who doesn't make some personal sacrifices in the summer and report in condition will find it almost impossible to make the starting eleven.

Most players agree that the most demanding and wearying part of practice is the wind sprint. Some coaches use the wind sprint (where players divide by positions and run several 50-yard dashes) early in the practice session while the players are comparatively fresh. They can get a better idea of the relative speed of their players.

We use wind sprints, not as a speed gauge, but as a conditioner, and we use them at the tail end of practice.

Defensive Mechanism

Among other changes in the sport is the more intelligent use of defense.

I can remember some people here in our own Southwest Conference talking about the first time they ever used a 5-3 defense and what a big change this was to football. Well, goodness knows, teams don't take just one defensive alignment and make one set charge the way they once did. Those teams of yore got pretty salty with that one standard rush, but now you can't tell what a defense will do just by what alignment it uses.

Defense now uses stunting linemen and looping linemen, linebacker keys, penetrating charges, control charges, and whatall.

Defense now plays down-and-distance more intelligently. If the play is third down and eight yards needed, they'll give and sag and let you run for four or five. But they don't want you throwing that forward pass. On short yardage, they'll jam up and come at you a little more directly. The defense is ever striving to create the third-down-and-six situation, wherein the offense must make six yards on third down or be forced to kick.

Different defensive charges represent a major change in today's game. If a coach considers his team outmanned, he may turn to a gambling defense, switching to a nine-man line on running situations, using a safetyman as a charging linebacker, inventing all sorts of off-brand alignments to create the bad play. He wants to force the other team out of its favorite offense, into something less familiar. And if these gambling defenses click, they may cause all sorts of headaches to the stronger team. If the defensive gamblers guess wrong on one play, it may easily go for a touchdown. But at least the more intelligent use of defense and the varied pattern of alignments and charges have done much to equalize and complicate the game.

Under the Punt

Another example of vastly improved defensive technique is punt coverage. Punt returns will kill you before a minnow can swim a dipper.

During my playing days at Oklahoma, we had fantastic success with punt returns. This was due largely to the fact that Coach Wilkinson spent many hours rehearsing the returns. I don't think other people were spending as much time covering kicks as we were spending in practicing returns.

We used two safeties, Jack Mitchell and myself, and we had picked up the crisscross maneuver from Texas A&M, after Marion Flannigan had shoved a punt down our throats in a 1946 game. After one safety caught the ball, he would run laterally toward the other safety and either hand off to him or fake a handoff. Each would make for the sidelines, looking for a blocking wall of friends.

Oklahoma had marvelous success with the crisscrossing safeties. In 1948, with Mitchell doing most of the returning, we set a national record. And those returns often meant the difference in a tight game and a topheavy score. We went up to play Kansas in 1948 in what was supposed to be a tight afternoon. We ran three punts back that day and it was a 60-7 game. That same year, Missouri came to Norman and they pushed us around in the first half. But Mitchell broke in on a couple of long punt returns in the second half and we wound up on a 41-7 end. We had so much punt return success that teams finally flatly refused to kick to us.

Now the reason those returns were so good was that teams were punting from a *tight* formation. The punter was only nine or ten yards back and the line was tightly bunched in front of him. The linemen had to stay and protect the punter longer because he was so close to the rushers. Then, when the blockers finally released their men and headed downfield, they came in a bunched-up wad, mainly because they started in a bunched-up wad.

If we could set up a wall of blockers and outflank that wall of down-rushing tacklers, then the safety man could scoot over behind that wall near the sideline and skip to the end zone while reading *Esquire Magazine*.

The Spread Punt Formation

Here is another example of the progress of football. Teams started using the spread punt formation. They stationed their kickers 13 yards behind the line, spaced their linemen over a wider area. Now all the linemen had to do was bump their rushers, straighten them up, and then release and flee downfield. The punter had more time because he was farther removed from the rushers.

The coverage was wider spread because the kicking team started from a spread formation in the first place, covering a much bigger portion of the field than the old balled-up tight formation.

Receiving teams will still establish that wall of blockers on one side or the other, but now the onrushing tacklers are spread all over the field. They seldom can be outflanked. They look for that wall of blockers and some of them will sift behind it and mess up the playhouse.

The Road Ahead

Coaches are often asked about the trend of football. Is it showing any pattern? What sort of styles or formations will the future bring?

Frankly, most of us are too busy trying to keep up from day to day to worry about trends.

I do think there is the possibility that the Split T formation will come back into vogue. Everything runs in a cycle. It seems as if the defense is always chasing the offense, and just as it catches up, the offense goes to some other formation. We've been playing the eight-man defensive front (the 6-2 and 5-3) for several seasons. We're concerned, along with other coaches, that if everyone goes back to the eight-man front and stays with it, the Split T will be popularized again.

The Split T was the offense that drove the eight-man front out of business in the first place. The Split T hand-off, the keeper play and the pitch-out—those three plays—broke the back of the eight-man front.

Then along came the nine-man front: five linemen and four linebackers, or six linemen and three linebackers. This was devised to stop the quick-striking Split T and was successful in doing so. Along came the Wing T, utilizing the flanker back, and it sent the nine-man front into mothballs. Now the eight-man front has come back in style to combat the Wing T. So it's logical to presume that the Split T will return to stab the eight-man front.

Of course, much depends upon rule changes. The trend seems to be back toward unlimited substitution. Right now we play under a strange hybrid set of rules, allowing full team substitution when the ball is dead, except on fourth down and on downs when the ball changes hands. I don't think this will change the game much from the style most coaches are used to. Defense will still be the key factor in winning games. Should unlimited substitution make a full return, there will be more specialists used, of course.

The rules that go into effect in 1963 may prove a handicap to teams like Army and LSU and Arkansas who use the three-team system: the offensive team specialists, the defensive specialists, and the both-ways team. It may be harder for a coach to juggle his specialist teams with time-outs trimmed to four per game, and the insertion of more than two subs prohibited on two downs out of a series. The new rules seem to provide more confusion than anything else.

Games still will be won by material, however, and not by the rulebook.

Tomorrow's Rules

As far as future rules are concerned, they're anybody's guess. But if we must change some laws, there are certain sections of the book which I would alter.

I never have been in favor of the two-point conversion rule. Too much emphasis is placed on a three-yard play. The ball is put into play about 140 times during a game, roughly 70 times by each team. And yet here we are, picking out one of those 140 plays and saying this particular down counts two points, if you are successful in making three yards. Why should that much importance be placed on just one down of the 140?

A year of coaching Edmonton in the Canadian professional league convinced me that the U.S. game could certainly use a couple of pointers from up north.

Why Have a 20-Yard Penalty for a Touchback?

First, I have never understood why a defensive team is awarded a 20-yard gift when an offensive team punts over the goal line for a touchback.

Under Canadian rules, any punt over the goal line that is not run back into the field of play by the safetyman counts as one point for the offensive team. This is called a *rouge*. In Canada, the goal posts are on the goal line and the end zones are 25 yards deep. If you are the attacking team and your offense becomes stalled on the 10-yard line, you may punt the ball as hard as you can, out of the end zone or out of the stadium. You get a point as a premium for advancing the ball down close to the enemy goal line. If your punt lands in the end zone, the safetyman must successfully run it back out across the goal line, or you get one point.

If you march down the field and score a touchdown, you get six points.

If you march down the field close enough to kick a field goal, you get three points, not quite as hard to do as to score a touchdown.

If you march down the field close enough to punt the ball over the goal line and tackle the safetyman in the end zone, or kick it completely over the end zone, you get one point. It's just a single point, but still it is some sort of award for advancing the ball into enemy territory.

Now in our U.S. game, if we move the ball inside enemy territory and kick it over the goal line, we get penalized 20 yards. That is, the opposing team gets possession of the ball on its 20-yard line without doing one darn thing to get it there. We are penalized for getting the ball *too* close to your goal, or because our kicker boots the ball *too* well!

It's the only time in football when a team is awarded something for doing nothing. The defending team is actually given 20 yards for refusing to play, refusing to catch the punt.

We tell our Texas safetymen to stand on the 10-yard line and if the punt goes over their heads, forget it. Two things can happen. A fumble, for one. And, too, chances are that the ball will bounce into the end zone and we collect our 20-yard gift. If the safetyman catches the ball on his five, then he's got to run it out 15 yards to break even. And a 15-yard punt return is exceptional the way coverage is today.

So we, as the receiving team refuse to gamble. We stand there and do nothing and get 20 yards for it. Maybe socialism has infiltrated football.

Now I don't advocate the *rouge* system of giving the one point. For one thing, our goal posts are located just 10 yards back of the goal line. Our end zones are just 10 yards deep and it would require more stadium reconstruction in order to arrange 25-yard end zones. Too expensive.

What I do argue is this: Don't give the receiving team 20 yards. When a punt goes over the goal line for a touchback, bring it out to the *five-yard* line only.

I guarantee that if a punt touchback came out only to the five, you'd see some Texas safetymen scrambling around and trying to catch the football and get it the dickens out of there. At the five-yard line, the cat is still on our backs. We're playing around with dynamite with the ball on our own five. We can't operate the way we could with the ball on the 20.

When a team rightfully gains field advantage, I don't think it should be taken away from it when its punt goes over the goal.

Don't Let 'Em Up

When I came back from Canada after the 1953 season, I went to the *Orange Bowl* game between Maryland and Oklahoma. It was an exciting game, excellently played. But I sat there in the stands and noticed something about U.S. football I had never realized before.

Just when the game got to a fever pitch and the crowd was all excited, when a team got on the move, and the band was playing and everybody yelling—somebody would call time out. The most thrilling part of the game would be soused in a bucket of ice water. It spoiled much of the enjoyment for the spectators.

In Canada, there are no time-outs.

If a player is hurt, he is carted off the field, a substitute rushed in and the clock is started right then, as soon as he reports.

Of course, there would be a lot of ramifications if we ever decide to do away with time-outs. But I had never realized what an injustice to the spectators, when you cut right into the most exciting part of the game with a two-minute interruption when nobody does anything.

In boxing, when you get an opponent a little groggy and on the ropes, he can't blow a whistle and say, wait a minute, you have the advantage now. Stop, I want to rest and regroup.

Basketball is the same way. A team gets going strong and a player pumps in a couple goals and suddenly, there's a time-out which kills all the action. I believe a rule eliminating time-outs would liven up our game.

Modern Pioneers

Whoever said there's nothing new under the sun wasn't a football coach. Some people say there's been nothing new in football for the past 20 years, but I beg to differ. The game is a continuing story of progress and new techniques and ideas. We say that defenses and offenses run in cycles, and this is true to a large degree. But each time the cycle comes around, there are a few new facets attached.

Football pioneers were daring, as are all pioneers. When John Heisman threw the first forward pass, in 1895, he was retreating, trying to find room to punt before the Georgia forwards buried him in the turf of Atlanta's Brisbane Park. But the stubborn Heisman recognized the potential of his new weapon and he plugged at the rulesmakers until they accepted it, 11 years later.

Bob Zuppke originated the modern huddle and was roundly censured for it. He used the spiral pass from center for a decade before others copied it. Bob Neyland introduced the run-option pass. There have been hundreds of football pioneers and there will be countless more.

My point is this: there are still new footballisms to be discovered and exploited. And the very worst *possible* excuse for shying away from something new, is "If it's good, somebody would have done it before."

Unwittingly, I was thrown into that sort of situation

when I went to Canada to coach professional football. They asked what system I would use, and I told them the Split T because it was the only thing I knew. I wasn't familiar with the professional techniques. I didn't know enough about the passing game and the pro-type game to try to coach it. There was no choice.

The Split T was sound football and there wasn't much reason why it shouldn't go, but I was greeted with the old cry, "If the Split T is all that good, how come somebody hasn't used it before up here?" Fortunately, the Split T went very well indeed at Edmonton. And it would have been successful in Canadian football all the time, probably, if someone had been forced into using it as I was.

A coach must be confident and aggressive, just as he expects his players to be. This doesn't mean he should be overbearing and cocky, for that's the surest method to get run over by an unidentified truck. But he must have belief in himself, his staff and his system. He must meet his problems more than halfway.

That famous old philosopher, C. Stengel, warned of the other consequences when he said, "Lotta people lose because they stand around waiting for something to happen. And it usually does." And it usually ain't good.

Pride in a Losing Coach

Also, perhaps there was something left out, in the previous discussion of pride and desire. It doesn't pertain only to players. Some of that pride and desire also must be draped around the coaches.

One truth recognized by all coaches is that the best coaching jobs, the hardest work, often comes during the losing seasons. Oklahoma, for example, made a tremendous comeback in 1961. They lost the first five games, then won the last five. I believe that was probably the best coaching job Bud Wilkinson has ever done at Norman, more so than when the *Sooners* were winning 40 straight. I felt our best job at Texas was in 1960 when we were 3-3 and then won the last four games.

Certainly it's just as easy for a coach to have his spirits down as for a player. You lose three or four games in a row and all sorts of doubts move in. You really might be doing a splendid job as coach, but simply be out-manned. Doubts seep in and eat away inside your noggin until you begin to wonder if your team isn't being outcoached.

A coach may begin to feel that somebody is outsmarting him, or that maybe his staff isn't getting as much production out of his squad as other staffs. Or maybe he feels that he's losing the personal touch, that he's not getting the instructions across to his players as well as he once did.

This is indeed a tragedy.

Humility in the Winning Coach

A winning coach is sometimes inclined to become oversold on his techniques or his system. He may feel that he's outsmarting his opponents if he wins.

But that's not nearly as bad as for a coach to lose confidence in what he's doing. To me, it is more disastrous. All of us are inclined, after we've had moderate success with the Split T or the single-wing or the eight-man front, to become firm believers in our own theories. Maybe the success is based solely on having better players than the other guy. We have a tendency, however, to think our particular system is the *only* system.

As wrong as that feeling is, it is still worse for a losing coach to feel downtrodden and inferior. To say to himself, well, we're just not doing as good a coaching job as Ole Miss, Georgia Tech, or Arkansas or somebody else. It could easily be that the coach just doesn't have enough player muscle at his command.

Confidence is contagious. So is a lack of confidence.

chapter four

Without Desire —Disaster

You've been sitting there reading for quite a few pages without realizing a world record was being established right before your eyes. Already several thousand words on college football have gone past without a single mention of "desire." This probably is enough to get me booted out of the brotherhood, because this particular term is just as important to a coach's vocabulary as "block," or "run," or "eat."

Desire is that cold fury burning inside a football player that makes him want to beat the other fellow. A player doesn't just acquire it; he doesn't wake up one morning and find himself broken out with desire like the chicken pox. He is born with it, for all humans are born with some degree of competitive urge. Football desire, to be sure, is built on pride and on effort, but it also has more impressive qualities, forged thus by raw combat, than either of these.

Deep Desire Can Be Seen

Some people believe you can actually see it. An offensive halfback, waiting for the snap, may see it in a defensive end who's positively quivering with eagerness to dash across the line of scrimmage and clobber somebody.

I've heard baseball men tell young pitchers, "When you get that ball back from the catcher, don't turn your back and look all around the outfield, trying to appear nonchalant. Grab that ball! Pound your glove! Glare at the hitter! Make him believe that you just can't wait to throw him the next pitch. You can scare him by just looking eager."

Tommy McDonald, the pepperpot halfback at Oklahoma and later a great pass receiver for the Philadelphia *Eagles,* was so charged with desire that it was obvious even to the untrained eye.

In college, Tommy would carry the ball, be tackled, literally fight his way out of the pile, sprint back to the huddle and prance up and down with impatience to run again. You can imagine how that picture would set with some big tackle, tired and sweaty in the fourth quarter, dragging himself back to a defensive position. "Why, that little so-and-so is still fresh and eager," he thinks. "What's the use? I couldn't catch him if I tried."

Red Grange cites Bronko Nagurski as the perfect example of desire, a dedicated lover of physical contact.

"He weighed about 245 when we played with the *Bears* and he ran his own interference," said Red. "If you played in the opposing secondary, you didn't have to worry about catching Nagurski. He'd look you up and go out of his way to give you a chance."

Close Your Eyes and Listen

Other people hold that you can actually hear desire, that it has a flat, ugly sound to it.

Bob Zuppke once was surveying an Illinois scrimmage when a player yelled, "Hey, coach, did'ja see that tackle I just made?"

"I don't look for tackles, son," said Zuppke. "I *listen.*"

A Texas sportswriter swore he could stand on the sidelines, shut his eyes and identify tackles made by E. J. Holub, All-America linebacker at Texas Tech and later a professional standout. "When Holub hits somebody, it has a distinctive sound," said the writer. "It sounds like a crate of curtain rods falling three floors and hitting flat on the sidewalk."

Desire Is the Constant Factor

However, there are cases of mistaken identity when you start looking for desire on a team.

Sometimes, in the fourth quarter, a team may simply appear in bad physical condition. Fans may complain that this particular squad hasn't been worked hard enough. In reality, the squad may be in better physical shape than the other team, but be lacking in desire. This team may be dragging back and forth and looking wistfully at the scoreboard, and the ailment won't be in their arms or legs.

I'd much rather have a team in bad condition with good morale, than in good condition with bad morale. It's much better, however, not to have to make that choice. (Nothing wrong with a little dash of greed in this case.)

Hate Your Neighbor

Desire has been defined as a sort of temporary hate for your opponent.

One of the greatest practitioners in this category was a fellow named Wild Bill Zock, a Canadian plumber who played for Edmonton the one season I coached there. I was 29 years old and it was my first head coaching job and I wasn't too sure of myself in many departments. I turned the job of arousing the team over to Wild Bill.

He was a giant of a fellow, 38 years old, and he must have been a tremendous physical specimen in his younger days. I made him squad captain and he assured me, "Don't worry, kid, I'll take care of everything."

Wild Bill would arrive for practice in his working clothes, house shoes, big wide suspenders and a longhandled undershirt. Before a game, he'd climb into his football uniform and find a piece of chalk. Then he'd go all over the clubhouse, writing "You gotta hate 'em" on walls, floors, mirrors, benches, lockers, or anything else.

He practiced this theory a bit too much to be entirely practical, however. Wild Bill was a guard and if he blocked a man in front of him, he'd still be down on him, whomping him several seconds later, when he should have been on his feet and running to where the action was. But Wild Bill had as much desire as any man I've ever seen.

After our 1957 Texas team upset Texas A&M 9-7, Bear Bryant went on his television program shortly after the game and explained, "Well, they just hated us worse than we hated them."

No Price Tags on Desire

I learned several lessons from that one year in Canada. It was a new experience in several different ways. It was my first job as a head coach. Some of my players were older than their coach. I had never been around professional football before, never even seen a game. But it didn't take long to learn that football desire is *football desire,* regardless of where it's played or the amount of the paycheck. You don't buy desire or pride or effort with a checkbook.

You've heard people speak of a college player, "When he turns pro and starts playing for money, he'll really bear down."

Balderdash. If a player, unrecognized in college, becomes a good pro, there must be other factors involved. Maybe he is happier in his new surroundings. There are cases when a player can go to one college and not do well, when if he had chosen another, he'd be outstanding. It might be that the player now just plays offense as a pro, or just on defense. It may be that he had personal problems in college or worries about finances or studies.

But I'm convinced that the money has nothing to do with it. Just by paying a boy, I don't think you can get him to give that big effort or make that necessary sacrifice to be a winning player. Real top drawer pros don't say to themselves: I'm going to play well today, so I can get a better contract next year. After they're on the field, then good old human nature takes over and the desire to beat the other fellow shoves those paychecks into the closet, forgotten for the time being. This element of desire in a player just doesn't go on and off like a refrigerator light. It must be a constant blaze.

Shoot the Works on Every Play

We try to impress upon our squad that football is really just like Russian Roulette. Most of the time, the firing pin clicks on an empty chamber but you never know when the big bang is coming.

It's our theory that close games are decided by four plays or fewer. You can choose five "key" plays and turn around the result of a really one-sided game. But take an ordinary game where the two teams are fairly even, and the outcome usually will be decided by fewer than five plays.

Yet there will be approximately 140 plays during the game. Only four of those will be the difference between the winner and the loser.

But our point is: YOU NEVER KNOW WHEN THAT BIG PLAY IS COMING UP.

We might put the ball in play 15 times and nothing of major consequence happens. The spectators may be dozing and the cheerleaders swapping telephone numbers and then, on a simple routine play, the bomb hits the siesta.

Any coach can think of many examples. Here's one that happened in 1958, in the Texas-Oklahoma game. Texas had a two-point lead, 8-6, in the last seven minutes of the game and it looked as if we might break the *Sooners'* six-year death grip on the rivalry.

From our own 24-yard line, quarterback Bobby Lackey called a sane, conservative play, a simple handoff to fullback Mike Dowdle in a drive at the middle.

But here comes your Russian Roulette. Dowdle took the ball and wheeled into the crowd and *Sooner* guard Jerry Thompson greeted him with hurricane force. The ball squirted from Dowdle's clutch and lolled, for just a split-second, on his hip. Another Oklahoma guard, Jim Davis, picked the plum and breezed past Lackey as if he were late for supper. Suddenly we were behind 8-14 because of a lightning bolt on a safe routine play. (Fortunately, Texas found a few bolts of its own in the last few minutes and squirmed out with a 15-14 win.)

But it gave us a text for future sermons. You don't know when those key plays will arrive any more than a hog knows it's Sunday.

In the Texas-Texas *Aggie* game of 1959, the *Aggies* had a short yardage situation 11 times during the game, third or fourth down with short yardage needed.

They were successful on 10 of those occasions. Only one time they failed, but that was on fourth down on the Texas one-yard line! That was the difference in the ball game, and the difference in Texas going to the *Cotton Bowl* that year or watching somebody else play on television. Only once were the *Longhorns* successful in stopping the *Aggies* and that was the key play of the game.

There can be no vacation periods for that desire. When those few key plays arrive, we must make sure we have an influence on them. Therefore, every play must be considered a potential game-breaker. Every down must be played to the hilt.

Home Fires Stoked by Effort

Desire has to be an inborn quality, but there are different methods to kindle it and keep it burning. Development of pride, of course, is one way. Hard work is another.

The harder a young man works on a project, the harder it is for him to surrender.

It isn't hard for a boy who hasn't worked out during the summer; who's loafed through practice; who's dozed through the lectures—it's not difficult for him to give up. What's he losing? He hasn't put anything into the project, so he isn't losing anything.

But if a youngster has thought football all summer,

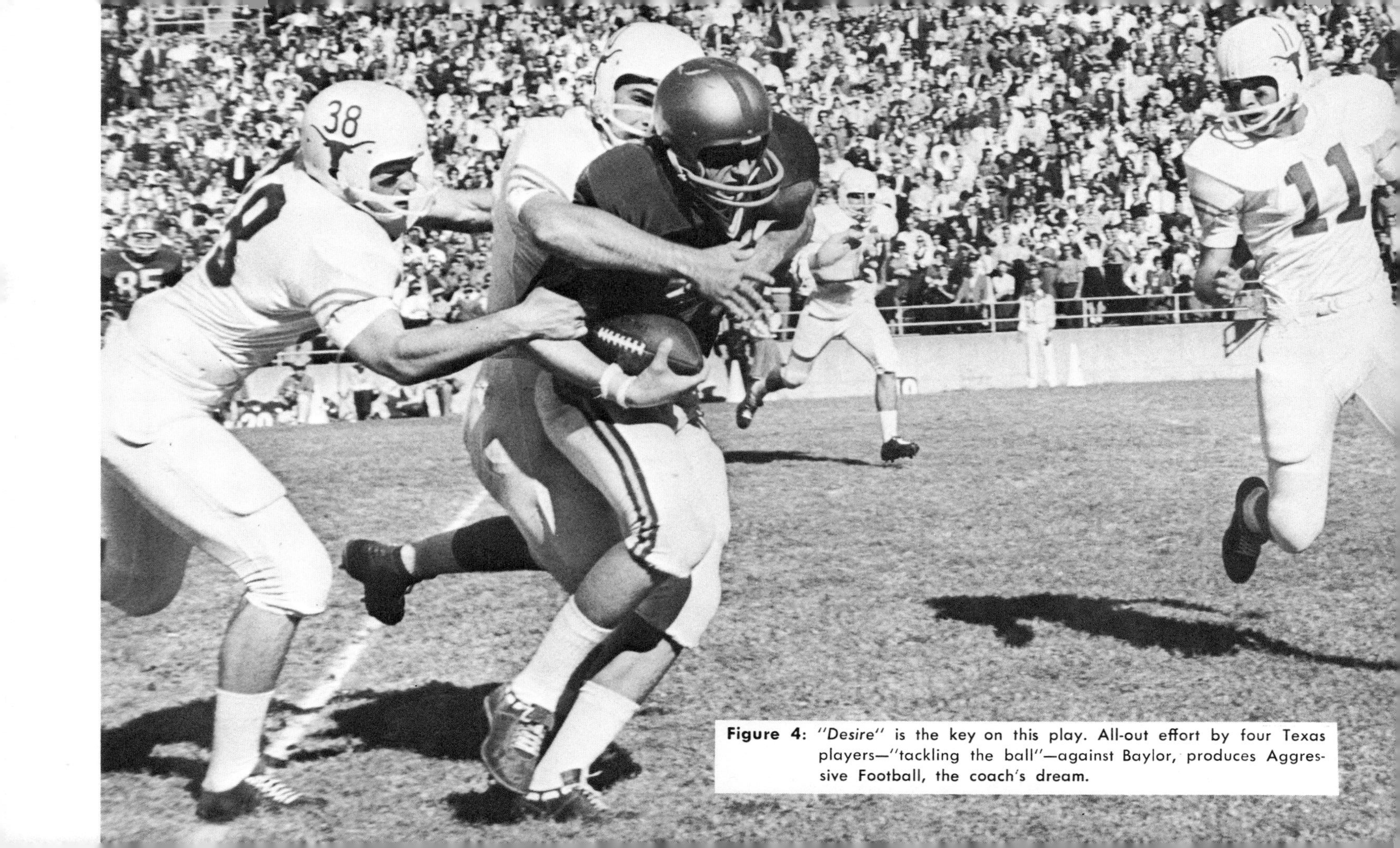

Figure 4: *"Desire"* is the key on this play. All-out effort by four Texas players—"tackling the ball"—against Baylor, produces Aggressive Football, the coach's dream.

worked hard and reported in good condition, then sacrificed, pushed and punished himself through the tough preseason drills, he has a pretty good stake in the game. He's much less apt to accept defeat.

Say, for example, a lad has labored long and hard and scrimped and saved his money and done without pleasure items so he can buy an automobile of his own. Another boy has a car given to him. Both of these cars are stolen. Which boy is hurt the most?

Defeat Is Mental

Every coach likes to impress on his squad that defeat is something that comes from within. Defeat must be admitted before it is a reality. This, of course, sounds like something from the pulpit and not from the locker room. But I like to hark back to a grammar school kid in Hollis, Okla., for example. His name was J. V. McEwing and we were walking home from school one day—we were in the third grade—when an older, larger boy bounced J. V. out and they had a fight.

J. V. took a drubbing and afterwards, we picked up his books and continued on down the sidewalk. I told him he had put up a good fight and there was no disgrace that he lost, because the other boy was older and bigger.

"He didn't whip me," J. V. said crossly.

"Sure, he did," I said. "There's no reason why he shouldn't."

"No, he didn't whip me. He's just a little ahead," he said stubbornly. "We're gonna fight again tomorrow."

Now, when you mention that defeat comes from within and there's no such thing as defeat until admittance, you'll hear some loud scoffers in the balcony.

"Pretty hard to convince a team behind by four touchdowns that it isn't defeated," you'll hear.

Correct. With four touchdowns behind and a few minutes remaining, I doubt seriously that anyone on field could convince himself that he wasn't already defeated. But somewhere in that game, some people on that team had already admitted defeat or they wouldn't be four touchdowns behind.

There are exceptions, of course. Teams are sometimes simply out-muscled. Teams sometimes are beaten on a fluke. But we don't like to admit those things.

Very possibly we are like the old Texan braggart who was interviewed by a national poll-taker on the economic situation.

"Do you think the recession will have political repercussions in Texas?"

"Son, we don't have a recession in Texas," said the oldtimer. "I'll admit, however, that our boom is worse than it's been in a good while."

Our Incentive System for Building Pride

1. *Grade as a Goad.* Most coaches use a grading system on game performances for a two-fold reason: to have a standard yardstick for evaluating their players, and to provide incentive for the players themselves. They want to put the bellows to that pride and desire.

Here, again, the game movies are the basis for the grades.

Usually, the assistant coaches divide this chore. The defensive coaches may grade all the defensive plays, and the offensive coaches vice-versa. Or one coach will simply take one player and follow him throughout the game, running the film back and forth until all the player's moves are clearly defined and recorded.

If the player gets his particular job done on this particular play, he is marked with a "plus"; if not, he gets a "minus." On some plays, he doesn't have the opportunity to help or hinder and he is not graded on those instances.

To arrive at a grade, the "plus" plays and the "minus" plays are added together and the sum is then divided into the "plus" number, the same way baseball batting averages are figured. Usually the offensive grades and defensive grades are figured separately, to tell if a player is more proficient in one than the other.

Some coaches have worked it down to a fine art; they'll say that a player must grade 60% or 62% to be a winning football player.

This is a little too fancy for me. We use a sort of grading system at Texas, but it doesn't involve percentages or a certain posted grade.

I once ran a test on this detailed grading, having four coaches study and grade a single player on 15 plays. There were four different grades. To me, the percentage grades involve too much personal opinion. Principally we want to know if the boy is giving a good effort, if he is playing better than the man in front of him, or below the man back of him.

The Texas assistant coaches study the films and mark a "Do" or "Don't" on each play's assignments. And they'll make notes on really special plays and really poor plays.

Then we'll talk about it. This usually is on a Monday following the game. For example, say we're discussing the tackle play in last week's game. Charlie Shira will give a report on how the tackles played defensively, who played better and who played worse. Jim Pittman will give the offensive report. Then I'll ask them individually if they think the lineup should remain as is, or if we should do some shifting around among first and second teamers. They decide whether we'll replace a tackle with the man below him.

If there is a difference on the offensive and defensive opinion, then I'll step in and decide on the tackle status for what I think is best for the team. In other words, if one tackle is better than his substitute on defense, the substitute is better on offense, then I have to make the decision. But this is rare. If the two tackles are equal, we leave the senior man on the first team. The junior second team tackle has to be better, not just equal, if he is to move ahead of the senior tackle.

2. *The Interception Chart.* While we don't post percentage grades, we do use several little incentive boosters on our bulletin board. For example, T. Jones, the defensive backfield coach, cuts out cardboard footballs representing each game on our schedule. These are labeled with the name of each opponent. Anyone who intercepts a pass has his name written on the football representing that particular game. These cardboard cutouts are hung in the training room corridor.

We also have a Recovered Fumble list posted on the board, and a Blocked Punt list.

3. *Plotting the Tackle.* Perhaps our most important defensive incentive was a brainchild of Mike Campbell, who coaches the defensive linemen and linebackers. He drew up a chart that shows the line of scrimmage and is graduated into five-yard, 10-yard and 15-yard lines on the defensive side of the line. Wherever a particular defender makes a tackle, a dot is drawn on his particular chart, in relation to the line of scrimmage. An unassisted tackle is represented by a star. A real exceptional tackle, an 18-karat gem, is emphasized by a red circle.

The chart also lists the total number of plays the defender experienced, the number of possible tackles at his position, the tackles he participated in, tackles on kickoff, punts and interceptions.

You can see from the actual tackle chart of linebacker Pat Culpepper in the 1961 Texas-Texas A&M *(Fig. 5)* that he had a tremendous afternoon. It is obvious that he stopped plays directed squarely at his right linebacker area, and also he roamed the field effectively.

You may find a linebacker's chart that shows plainly that he doesn't make any tackles except those right around him. It's real obvious to him, by looking at the chart, that he's not getting off his tail and getting in on plays that go a long way from him. You'll find another linebacker who seldom makes any tackles that are run straight at him, but he'll make tackles everywhere else. His chart will indicate that he's not facing the flow of traffic; he's not playing

A & M GAME

TACKLES ON:

PLAYER CULPEPPER

KICKOFF ● ★

PUNT ______

INTERCEPTION ______

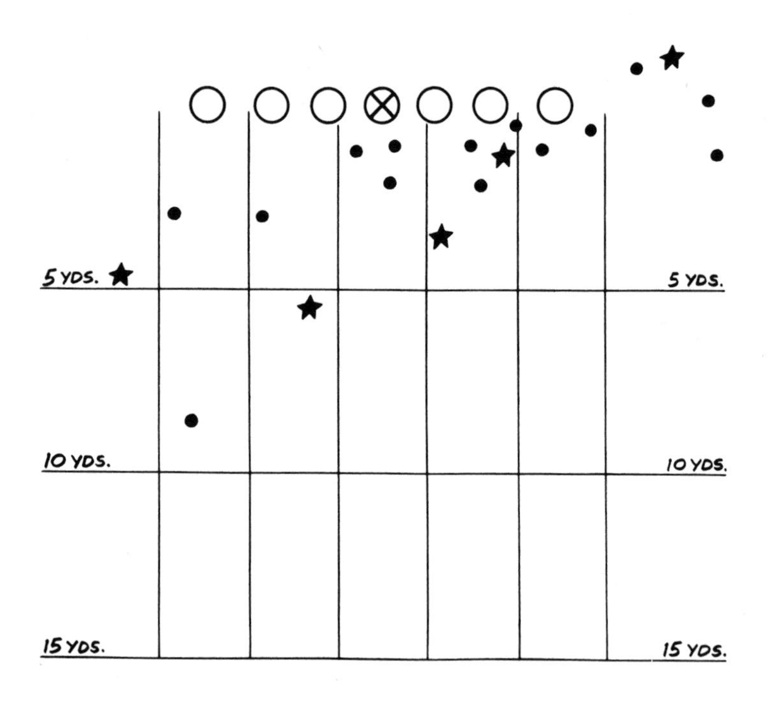

TOTAL PLAYS 41

NUMBER OF POSSIBLE TACKLES AT HIS POSITION 8

NUMBER OF TACKLES 19

Figure 5

solid enough right at home. When the offensive runs directly at him, he's soft.

A Proud Look at the Record

These tackle charts are posted. They are an incentive. You should see the players flock around the bulletin board on Monday afternoons.

This is a form of grading but, to us, it means more than to say, "Okay, Culpepper, defensively we're going to grade you 83% in last Saturday's game." What does that tell him? On this graph he can readily see where he's being efficient and where he is slack.

The Accent Is on Defense

We spend much more time charting and boosting the defensive work than we do the offensive. You don't have to encourage a boy to catch a ball, or to run with the ball. Defensive players don't always get the sort of recognition they deserve.

Posted Reminders

Locker room signs, I suppose, are as much a part of football as the pump and lacing. They are used to stress a purpose, furnish fuel for desire or simply to remind the young men of their pride.

We use them. Frankly, I don't know their value. Some of them are original; some are derived from other quotations or speeches. We change them from year to year, depending on the type of season we had.

Our first year, a sign read: "Luck is what happens when preparation meets with opportunity."

Another season, after we had won several games with last quarter rallies, a sign was: "Our greatest glory is not in never falling, but in rising every time we fall."

Then, after a couple of successful years, there was a

new sign: "Texas' winning tradition will not be entrusted to the timid or to the weak."

The kids might laugh at them and poke fun, I don't know. But I do know they read them and remember.

Rene Ramirez was a rugged halfback and also a rugged individualist at Texas our first season there. He wasn't exactly the rah-rah type and something less than a firebrand in practice. But several years after he left Texas, we were sitting together one night at a high school game. One of the teams scored and a nearby fan stood up and yelled, "How about that for dumb luck!"

Ramirez nudged me and winked.

"Luck is what happens when preparation meets with opportunity," he said, just as verbatim as could be.

chapter five

Out on the West Coast, the byword is "Movies Are Better Than Ever." Well, sir, in the summer of 1961, the same was true in the general vicinity of Austin, Texas, and I don't mean the films where Audie Murphy rides off into the sunset after saving the homestead. The Longhorn coaching staff had itself another type of movie hero.

We sat around in air-conditioned film rooms and ran the game movies of 1960 over and over. And then we would look at each other silently, with universal conviction that we had an amazing weapon on our hands if we could discover best how to load and shoot it.

A New Dog

James Saxton was the weapon's name and he was a

The Flip-Flop: New Dog, Old Tricks

spindly whippet with steel legs split up to his breastbone. He could run like small-town gossip, although his compass sometimes went batty.

By giving the scales a friendly nudge, James could persuade them all the way up to 165 pounds. He was a crew-cut youngster, with sideburns and a high-pitched voice and he looked about as much like an All-America halfback as the late Big Daddy Lipscomb resembled a Rockette.

Saxton had started his college career as a quarterback, but we had moved him to halfback for his junior season.

He was Hairbreadth Harry every time he carried the ball. He was as apt to run 50 yards as five because James was a skittery, fluttering runner who could find daylight where none existed. His only trouble was that he wasn't a hardy individual. He was compared to a rubber balloon

Figure 6: The "spindly whippet" in action! James Saxton's speed and spring gave us the idea for the Flip-Flop offense. Here Jim uncoils in the 1961 Texas-Rice game.

blown up and turned loose, swirling and darting helter-skelter all over the room until finally collapsing with a whoosh.

Newspapermen called him Jackrabbit Jim, because of an earlier history of chasing down rabbits in East Texas pastures. Some said he ran like a knuckleball. Others compared him to a waterbug, with a cottonmouth moccasin in pursuit. He was a colorful youngster, and he averaged better than five yards each time he carried the ball his junior year. He was our leading ground gainer in 1960 with 436 yards.

Saxton certainly was no surprise to the coaching staff. We didn't just discover him in the background of game films, like a movie extra who is suddenly chosen for stardom. We had been delighting in his wild talents for two seasons.

But as we studied and re-studied those game films, one fact began to scream for attention:

Saxton was not being used to best advantage.

He wasn't durable enough to play most of the game, to block and play defense. So our first conclusion was that this constant scoring threat should be running with the football while he was in the game.

He shouldn't be blocking for somebody else. We wanted to stick that football under his arm every possible chance and tempt a little heart failure from the opposition.

And that's how the Flip-Flop offense was born.

Old Tricks

It wasn't a new idea at all. But someone tacked a fancy nickname on it in our instance, and it started growing like Topsy. It became a surprise even to our coaching staff.

But back to Saxton. We wanted the football in his hands. To heck with the idea of his playing left halfback and carrying the ball on one play, flanking on another play, being a pass receiver on another, blocking on another, decoying on another. So along came the idea, out of one of those hot weather bull sessions, of installing a tailback plan.

Take the left halfbacks and make tailbacks out of them, so that they would always line up alongside the fullback, in a ball-carrying position. Like the pros—have a permanent running halfback.

The right halfbacks, therefore, would become wingbacks. They would be wingbacks on the right side when the formation was Strong Right; they would move to the left side when the formation was Strong Left.

This, of course, would put Saxton and his fellow left halfbacks in business on every play, especially pointing the Saxton potential at the end sweeps and off-tackle plays.

Then we shifted attention to the ends, while still just kicking the idea around. Since the wingback must do double-team blocking with the ends on the all-important sweep plays, why not pair him with the same end every time?

Instead of having a right end and a left end, why not use a constant strongside end who would shift with the wingback, either to the right or left side of the line? Then it would simplify our coaching (a constant aim). We could keep the same two positions together all the time and teach the blocking to the same combination of players. We would make a two-man team out of the wingback and the strongside end. Result—togetherness.

Then, we could take the weakside end and make him our specialized pass receiver.

In a subsequent session, one of our assistant coaches (I don't remember who) made another suggestion. The center, quarterback, and fullback play the same location all the time. With the changing of our halfbacks and ends, we had switched everybody but the guards and tackles to the strongside-weakside plan. Why not switch them also? A further simplification.

So we just decided to change the whole bunch—halfbacks, guards, tackles, ends—into the strongside-weakside plan. (The location of the wingback, of course, determines the strong side.)

Long Distance Advice

Now this was nothing new, as I said. Several, even numerous, coaches had employed the strongside-weakside theme for years. So I yelled for help.

These staff talks were in August before practice started in September. We had not received benefit of spring work on the idea, because we simply hadn't thought of it then. But Saxton's senior season was arriving with breakneck speed, and if we were going to the party, we had to get dressed. So I decided to call some coaches who had experience in this plan.

Jim Owens at Washington had some success with switching his linemen from one side to the other. He used an unbalanced line, so it wasn't exactly the same. I called Jim, and I called Bob Woodruff, the assistant coach at Tennessee and former boss at Baylor and Florida. Bob, of course, sprang from Tennessee stock and he had experience with this strongside-weakside business before Jim and I were big enough to play in the backyard.

I asked them both this question: Would it be a mistake to go into this type of offense without having the benefit of spring practice?

Both said they didn't think so, because it was a move of that everloving simplification. If you're simplifying (they said), you can do it anytime. If you want to install something more complicated than your present plan, then you better take the spring drills to work on it.

Both Jim and Bob assured us that August was not too late.

The Problem of the Huddle Muddle

Then, we were faced with the problem of breaking from the huddle when the formation was Strong Left, without a traffic problem.

When the formation strength was to the right, then it was simply the routine way, because our Strong Side linemen would be on the right side of the huddle. However, if a Strong Left formation were called, the right side of the huddle would have to cross over to the left side of center to line up, and vice-versa.

Again, this is no new problem. Several single-wing teams using the strong-weak scheme break from the huddle in a long serpentine stream which weaves up to the line in single file. UCLA used this plan and many Tennessee-schooled coaches do.

However, I could remember when we played against this huddle-breaking method. We would also have a strong-side and weakside defense, so we'd stand in a defensive huddle. And when the other team would start that serpentine winding, our line would weave along with them and our strongside linemen would have plenty of time to drop into position against the opponent's strong side.

That method of huddle-breaking took too much time for our fancy. So we got out the blackboard and scratched around on it for awhile and came up with a crisscrossing method.

In other words, if the Strong Left formation were called, the center would break out of the huddle first, of course. Then the right guard would follow, crossing in back of the center to his position immediately to the center's left. The left guard would hesitate momentarily and cross behind the right guard to his spot right of the center. Then the tackles and ends would follow suit, with the strongside man always making his crossover first, and his weakside counterpart crossing just on his heels.

The wingback would just skip over to the left side, the tailback and fullback fall into place naturally, and the quarterback waits briefly and is the last man to line up after the traffic ahead of him has cleared.

After we drew off this crisscrossing plan on the back-board, we were anxious to see if it would work smoothly.

Now this may seem as though undue importance was put upon a simple maneuver like breaking the huddle, but we considered it most important to break quickly and smoothly, get up to the line and get the play underway before the defense had a lot of time to think it over.

So we gathered up the coaching staff, enlisted Bob Rochs and Al Lundsteadt from the athletic ticket office, and went to the gymnasium floor to try it out.

We did it easily; nary a head was bumped. We figured if all of us oldtimers could do it, the players could handle it like a ballet line.

Sure enough, they did. When fall practice started, we had them walk through it a couple times, then turned them loose and let it alone. After they stepped on each other's toes a few times, they learned quickly.

So, with this method, we were able to line up either Strong Right or Strong Left, quickly and smoothly, and the defense had no extra time to think things over.

The Chief By-Product Was Simplicity

Mind you, the primary reasoning behind this switch in offense was *James Saxton*. We had sort of an unquenchable curiosity to see how many times he could visit the end zone. But, of course, we still were going to use the same offense, regardless of whether Saxton was in the game.

Then, the longer we worked with it, the clearer the by-products became, and the chief accomplishment of the Flip-Flop was that it simplified signals for everybody.

1. *Fewer Plays to Learn.* The linemen had just five plays to learn all year, five blocking assignments at the point of attack. Of course, they had downfield blocking assignments when the play went to the other side, but that chore is just a matter of hustle, not of expert timing and execution.

The strongside tackle, for example, blocked the same way on a strongside sweep whether it was right or left, because he was always stationed in the same comparable position. This sliced his blocking assignments in half.

We started the season with that simple assortment

of plays (with the linemen having only five assignments to learn) and were fortunate enough to be able to stick with them all year.

Truthfully, when we started that first Flip-Flop season, we didn't feel as though we had enough plays. But California was our opening opponent that year, and the *Golden Bears* had no way of knowing that we were going to use the Flip-Flop, or just how few plays we were going to run. So we thought we'd go into the season with these few plays and make adjustments from there.

Well, against California we moved the ball well. Our next opponent was Texas Tech and the *Raiders* had no guarantee that we wouldn't add new plays for them. So we didn't. The simple offense rocked along all right, and also through the Washington State game. We were averaging seven yards per play.

Then came Oklahoma, the big, big one. We thought, well, this is the time to put in some new plays. But by then, the staff and team were so confident that those few plays were the answer, they were reluctant to add anything else. When the halfway point of the season was reached, it was just like slapping the quarterback in the face to suggest putting in a new play.

Therefore, the first year of the Flip-Flop, we wound up with the identical blocking assignments in the *Cotton Bowl* game against Mississippi that we had in the first game of the season. This was something new for us, an about-face.

Heretofore, we had never taken the same play and blocked the same way for the full year. Not a single play. We'd change blocking assignments every week, according to the opponent, and it's a mystery why more of our players didn't turn completely cross-eyed. Our linemen must have had 25 different assignments to learn in previous seasons, where now we had only five.

2. ***Less Confusion—More Aggressiveness.*** Now, when you have just those few movements to learn, your execution becomes a crisp action and becomes sure of itself through constant repetition. A change in defense doesn't bother you.

It all comes back to what we mentioned earlier: less confusion.

If players have fewer assignments to learn, they can concentrate on blasting those guys on the other side of the line. They can be as aggressive as they darn well choose because they're sure of their movements.

3. ***Eliminated the Busted Signal.*** Of course, simplification not only pays off in aggressiveness, but also in lessening that prominent coaches' headache: the busted signal.

There is nothing that will knock the breath out of an offensive move like a goofed assignment, a forgotten duty. Confusion breeds these mistakes and it seems like a determined action to send a coach to an early grave. But the simpler the chores, the fewer the mental errors.

For example, in 1960 we averaged 9.6 busted assignments per game.

In 1961, under the new simplified offense, Texas averaged *only one* busted assignment per game.

This is pointed out more graphically by a comparison of actual scores out of actual possessions—a batting average, as it were, of a team's scoring efficiency.

A review of Texas' touchdown analysis of the four seasons before the Flip-Flop:

- 1957 team scored 21 times of 117 possessions for 18%.
- 1958 team scored 24 times of 137 possessions for 18%.
- 1959 team scored 29 times of 129 possessions for 22.5%.
- 1960 team scored 25 times of 116 possessions for 21.5%.

And then, along comes the Flip-Flop and its simpli-

Figure 7: This scene from the 1961 Texas-Baylor game pictures nicely the potential of the Flip-Flop as Saxton builds up momentum behind a wall of blockers.

fication (*i.e.*, fewer busted signals) and the analysis reads:

- 1961 team scored 44 times of 134 possessions for 33%.

Please let me repeat: I don't think the Flip-Flop offense is the answer to any particular problem. Not at all. You simply must have play execution, whether you're running the Flip-Flop, or the Flop-Flip, or the One-Eyed Jacks Wild. And, of course, you must have the material. The following year, 1962, pointed up that fact.

The Texas material that started the Flip-Flop could have run any offensive formation. That team could have been a successful Split T operation. The next season, however, we lost Saxton and Jack Collins and a fine-thinking quarterback, Mike Cotten, and we weren't as potent offensively. We scored just 28 times out of 141 possessions for a 20% efficiency, which was still better than some old averages. Our defense was chiefly responsible for a 9-0-1 season. In reality, that 1962 outfit that stressed defense and kicking was more our *type* of team than the explosive 1961 group.

And, speaking of successful Split T operations, our Flip-Flop offensive thinking is very similar to the thinking of the Split T. That formation ran only about three plays to either side. The Split T won with execution.

And that, of course, is the answer—executing the play against any defense you face and running it time after time after time until your offense has the ability to react and adjust to any defensive alignment.

The Brass Tacks of Flip-Flop

The Flip-Flop uses three basic plays: the pitchback sweep to the strong side, the option to the fullback wide to the weak side, and the trap up the middle. You mix in just enough off-tackle plays to keep folks at home in that territory. But those three basic moves place an adequate strain on the defense: wide to either side and up the chute.

The sweep is the most popular play, and it should be your big yardage gainer.

That first season, Texas was extremely lucky to have three fine tailbacks. As I said, the offense was constructed around Saxton, but once we changed the attack, we had to use the same offense regardless of who was running at tailback. We had two other lads at tailback who caused about as much damage as Saxton. And they were all three different types.

Saxton was a thin jitterbug; Jerry Cook was a big, smooth glider; Tommy Ford was a compact blaster. (They finished first, third and seventh, respectively, among Southwest Conference's leading rushers.)

You can see how the arrangement benefited Saxton. The year before, he had averaged 5.4 yards for a total of 436 for the season. Under the tailback plan, he averaged 7.9 yards for a total of 849 yards, the largest total ever reached by a University of Texas back. Yet he played less than half the time.

After our first four games, Saxton had averaged 11 yards per whack on 28 trips and had played but sparingly. Which led one sportswriter to speculate:

> Saxton may be the first player in history to make All-American and not play enough to earn a letter.

Cook and Ford both averaged better than five yards per rush. It doubtless will be a long time before any coach ever has three tailbacks of that particular combination; probably never again for me. A coach is entitled to that favor only once in a career.

The increase in the Texas yardage production after the Flip-Flop installation in 1961 may be seen below:

- 1958—2,409 yards, rushing and passing
- 1959—2,730 yards, rushing and passing
- 1960—2,500 yards, rushing and passing
- 1961—3,831 yards, rushing and passing
- 1962—2,860 yards, rushing and passing

Cart Before the Horse

The Flip-Flop represented a *flip-flop* in our coaching theories. Never before had we tried to change an offense to fit our material. Bob Zuppke used to say he'd look over his material and then decide on his formations. I've read of other coaches doing this. But I've never been that smart and I'm afraid I wouldn't be able to make all the pieces fit together.

Most coaches learn one offense, work up a strong belief in it, and then say, well, here it is, now let's find some people to run these plays.

However, it didn't take any Einstein to sit before those game movies and decide you wanted Saxton to run with the football every possible play he could, no matter how. We didn't start out with the Flip-Flop plays. We started out with the idea of getting the ball to Saxton with enough room for him to maneuver. The plays followed.

Always before (and perhaps again some time in the future) we have run the Split T and the Wing T and simply combed our squad for the players best suited to run those plays.

What About the Passing Game? People have asked this question: what if you were teaching a conservative chug-chug offense and you suddenly fell heir to a sensational passer and you were going to have his services for three varsity years? I'd think you'd stick with the same formations you had been running, but simply throw the ball more.

I might say this: we've always been a running team and I'm sure we will continue to be so. (We've been criticized for it, I might add.) But I've always felt that three things can happen to you whenever you throw the football, and two of them are bad. You can catch the ball, you can throw it incomplete, or have it intercepted. There are college coaches who argue that passing teams become lazy teams. That the passing yardage comes so easy, and the team finds it hard to buckle down and go for those three tough yards when they have to.

In other words, a passing team tends to neglect the hard-rock duties of blocking the other guys flat and running through their territory, because it's easier to throw over the other guys' heads—the path, as they say, of least resistance.

Coaches who believe in the "pro-type" offense for colleges will argue stoutly that pass protection blocking is the toughest part of football, that you can't be lazy and execute it well.

Passing coaches, to be frank, haven't exactly been overly successful in promoting their theories lately and some of them are rather sensitive about it. Woody Hayes of Ohio State is a man dedicated to free speech and he rubbed some tender skins raw a few years ago when he said, "A passer is beautiful to watch, but he'll get you beat every time." Which was a way of saying that passing teams do not win in college ranks.

Dutch Meyer, who coached two pretty fair chunkers at TCU in Sam Baugh and Davey O'Brien, once answered that question.

"There is the danger that a passing team becomes lazy," said Dutch. "A passing team might not crack down on running plays, because it feels like it can make yardage easier on passes. However, I don't think a passing team gets soft on defense. Back then [in the Baugh and O'Brien days], we just didn't spend as much time on defense in practice."

Passing* Is *Flashy, But . . . I have no wish to enter the argument, if there is one.

However, you may take the weekly statistical leaders around the country and see how they're doing in the won-lost department. Draw your own conclusions.

A few seasons back, one of our Southwest writers ran a check on a particular weekend. The top 10 passing teams in the country were playing at a .466 won-lost percentage. The 10 top rushing teams had a .824 percentage.

It was that same weekend that Dick Norman set so

many NCAA passing records for Stanford. He threw the ball 39 times in Stanford's game against California. He connected on 34 of those passes, an unbelievable percentage. Norman passed for a total of 401 yards.

Stanford lost the afternoon, 17-20, to California, a team that had been beaten eight times that year.

Earlier that same autumn, an Iowa passing ace named Olen Treadway completed 26 out of 41 passes against Wisconsin for a whopping 304 yards. Iowa lost, 16-25.

Maybe the "pro-type" attack is a better crowd-pleaser. Maybe it creates more excitement. Maybe, also, it's another case of the coat and the pants doing all the work, and the vest getting all the gravy.

Of course, most coaches don't measure the success of a passing attack by how many passes are completed. It's how many passes you complete when you *have* to complete them.

It's just like the theory on what makes a good double play combination in baseball. Not the number of double plays made during a season. It's how many double plays are made when they *have* to be made. That's your successful double play operation.

So it is with a passing attack, in my opinion. The Texas A&M team of a few years ago was a ripping, tough ground outfit built around the lunges of Jack Pardee and John David Crow and Lloyd Taylor, and the forward pass was supposedly a foreign weapon. The Aggies completed only about 30 passes all season long, but nine of them were for vital scores. A halfback would take a pitchout for a goal line sweep and then lob a fluttery dying quail into the end zone where some teammate would surround it. It led to a popular saying, "A&M can't pass a lick, except for touchdowns."

However, as far as passing teams are concerned, I must admit they cause us more preparation worry than any others. We're scared to death before we play a team like Baylor or Washington State because we don't see that passing offense often enough to be used to it. I'm not saying that the running coaches' way is the right way. Maybe it isn't. But a coach must teach what he knows and believes in, and all my experience has been with running teams.

The Impact of the Flip-Flop

But I digress; back to the Flip-Flop again. Since the offense met with a batch of national publicity, we were swamped with mail from all over the country, requests for literature and films and what not. We had more coaches visit our spring drills than ever before. At coaching clinics around the country, we were besieged with questions about this new offense, which was really about as new as whooping cough.

1. *The Most Popular Question Was This:* What if you lose a starting guard or tackle through injury? For example, say your No. 1 weakside tackle is hurt.

Normally, the solution would be to advance the third best tackle on the squad to the starting position, whether he be a right tackle or a left tackle by trade. This would still put your two best available tackles in the starting line-up.

But (under the Flip-Flop plan) maybe your third best tackle is a strongside tackle. He has specialized in strongside blocking, and now you want to move him to the No. 1 *weakside* tackle and have him learn new techniques in the middle of the season. What now?

That's the first question we're asked and that was the first question I asked Bob Woodruff when I called him to talk about switching linemen on that August day.

The answer: no sweat, no strain. It's no problem at all. The boy has such a small number of plays to learn after he changes to the other side, he has no trouble adapting. He's been used to blocking either right shoulder or left shoulder anyway, because he's been flip-flopping.

We had to make that particular change a few times that first season and I was surprised how fast the players picked it up. We've found out that it's simpler to coach the boy just one way and then change him if we have to; simpler than coaching him *both* ways from the beginning.

2. ***Another Frequent Question About the Flip-Flop:*** "I have two boys about equal as ball carriers and I hate to make a wingback out of one. Isn't there a morale problem if you take ball-carrying away from one of them?"

Well, some coaches might think that's a problem, but I don't. In the first place, your wingback also carries the ball on some plays, and he's also a pass receiver. Secondly, your guards don't carry the ball. Do you have to do a selling job on them to preserve their morale?

We had a halfback at Texas named Jack Collins who had a fine sophomore year and a rather disappointing junior season. We shifted him to wingback in his senior year and he enjoyed his very best season for us and everyone recognized it. You must be a team man to play winning football. Self-preservation may be the first law of nature, but it's way down the list of football laws.

People have asked us to name the chief requirement for the Flip-Flop offense. For example, must you have a goodly supply of exceptional runners for the tailback duties?

Of course, I think you must have good runners for any type of offense. To have a football team which is better than average, you must have someone who can scat when he gets the ball.

You don't really need any better runners or any more runners for the Flip-Flop than any other offense. As a matter of fact, you don't need as many! We simply take our better runners and put them at tailback. We let them perform their specialty.

It's the team that runs a mirrored offense that needs more runners. On the sweep to the right, the left halfback carries the ball and the right half goes to wingback. On the sweep to the left, the right halfback carries and the left half goes to wing. So you must have good runners as substitutes for them. Therefore, you need four good ball carries for the mirrored offense.

The Flip-Flop could get by with just two. A starter and

a replacement. If the mirrored offense had just two good runners, there would be no replacements and you'd have some mighty tired and inefficient young men on your hands in the fourth quarter.

Our tailbacks carry the ball roughly 52 percent of the time. This was the same percentage both our halfbacks totaled before the Flip-Flop was installed.

3. *Another Question:* Must you have more speed to run the Flip-Flop? Nope. You must have speed and good runners to run any offense. In the Split T, those halfbacks have to burn around the ends on the pitchout and they have to come a long way to get in position to take the ball. Speed is welcome, and even necessary, to run the Flip-Flop, but no more so than in any other offensive attack.

Defensing the Flip-Flop

Most opponents will use a straight solid defense against the Flip-Flop. A few will shift a man to your strong (wingback) side. However, when we scrimmage against ourselves, we play in balanced alignment. If you line up balanced, you're not creating a real weakness. If the defense is overbalanced toward the wingback, then it is inviting the option play to the fullback, wide to the weak side.

The Flip-Flop has the same basic thinking as the Split T as far as simple play execution is concerned. But it certainly doesn't look the same. In the Split T, a certain number of plays start off looking alike. The quarterback starts sliding down the line and the play can be a handoff, or the keep-and-pitch, or the option.

Our plays don't start out looking alike. We don't try to fool many people.

I know this must sound like a stuck needle, but I must keep repeating that a coach doesn't win with the Split T, or the Wing T, or the Flip-Flop or the spread. He wins with sharp execution of a few basic plays and good personnel. What's the old saying? You can't make good chicken salad with chicken feathers. Something like that.

The Source of "Flip-Flop" and Other Unlikely Nicknames

The name "Flip-Flop" was born in a newspaper interview, innocently enough, but I suppose it was responsible to some degree for the national attention the offense attracted.

Southwest football writers band together and spend a day in each of the eight camps during pre-season training. The photographers run wild and the reporters interview coaches and players and the entire day is turned over to the news media.

It was at one of these interviews that I mentioned casually that we were going to use a strongside line and a weakside line, and that they would crisscross coming out of the huddle.

I really hadn't thought it was too much of a story because certainly people had done it before. As I said, the Tennessee clan has used it, and the professionals have long used running backs and wingbacks.

Anyway the writers seemed excited about it, chiefly, I suppose, because Saxton was going to be lugging the ball more.

"What do you call this offense?" someone asked.

"I don't know," I answered. "We haven't called it anything."

The Wing T had been used before, so the writers discarded that as too drab. Then someone said, "Well, what it amounts to, is the line just flip-flops over, according to the strength of the formation, doesn't it?"

I said I guessed so, and the name *Flip-Flop* stuck. Had it been called the M140-Flanker-R, chances are you never would have heard of it outside the Austin city limits. But the sound of Flip-Flop had a bit of imagination to it and sportswriters always seem to be searching for that bit of color.

Several years ago Paul Dietzel reached into his psychology book and chose a brand for his third team. These lads were defensive specialists at Louisiana State, but Paul did not want to call them the third team. He wanted to hypnotize them into believing they were eleven feet tall and much superior to anything else in the neighborhood.

So he called them "The Chinese Bandits," and it was like dope. They wore the name like the Congressional Medal of Honor. In doing this, Dietzel launched a new era in nicknames.

Of course, the sports world has long been strewn with nicknames. We've had the *Four Horsemen* and the *Bronx Bombers* and the *Gas House Gang*. And then almost every individual who flirted with the headlines got himself all fancied up with something like *The Sultan of Swat, The Splendid Splinter, The Wild Bull of the Pampas*. And who can ever forget that melody called *The Crying Greek from Cripple Creek?*

But the practice seemed to have paled a bit until Coach Dietzel spanked life into its cheeks. Frank Broyles at Arkansas fell eagerly into line. He named all three of his teams with admirable imagination, like The Big Red and The Thundering Third and he tagged his fullback-linebacker as "The Monster." Now, several years later, the Arkansas defense which has a roving linebacker is called the Monster Defense and is used by many coaches.

Jerry Burns at Iowa may have set the record in defensive nicknames. The Iowa roving linebacker is called the Hawk. When he lines up on the left side, his next door neighbor is the Anchor End. The other is the Blood End. There also is a Blood Tackle and a Slant Tackle.

The middle defender, of course, is the Nose Man.

The left linebacker is Scrape, the right is Shuffle. There is a Strong halfback and a Squirm halfback. The safety, believe it or not, is called Safety.

Of course if the Hawk shifts to the right side, then Anchor becomes Blood and Scrape becomes Shuffle and Strong becomes Squirm—and some of us become quite dizzy.

But the nicknames are here to stay. The Flip-Flop gained national prominence, not because of its explosive results, but because its name is a form of advertising. And who says it doesn't pay to advertise?

In Colorado, there are 26 mountains taller than Pike's Peak. Name one.

chapter six

Several years ago a group of sportswriters was batting the football breeze with Frank Broyles up in the Arkansas hills.

Frank expounded on his theories of defense and the kicking game and finally he said, "In college football, you play first to tie, and then play to win."

The writers looked aghast. What kind of positive thinking was this? A tie is like leaving the Thanksgiving table after just one bite of the turkey leg. Object of the game is to win, win, win. Even Abe Martin, the TCU philosopher, has said, "A tie is just like kissing your sister."

A few days later, these same writers were telling me of Frank's conversation. When I agreed with him, they quickly gave me the fish eye and looked at each other with the universal puzzlement of what in the tomfool is this world coming to?

In Defense of Defense

If They Don't Score, They Can't Win

What Frank was saying, however, is the basic precept of football: You never lose a ball game if your opponent doesn't score.

Therefore, you first play to keep him from scoring. Then, you play to score yourself.

This is good, old, raw defensive thinking and it is certainly not the most popular feeling among the spectators in the stands. All the world loves a lover, but it is simply nuts about a gambler.

Sure, the people in the stands want you to be bold and aggressive with your offensive thinking. They like to

see you pass from your end of the field and run on fourth down in neutral territory. The average fan wants you to play for the win at all times; never settle for the tie. But there's a small difference.

The Fan Is Playing With Your Chips

The average fan has nothing to lose. If your team isn't successful in a gamble to win a game, the defeat doesn't hurt the spectators. They'll shrug and go on to their cocktail parties and have a big time and go back to their respective businesses on Monday. And you're left sitting there in the stadium with a big hole in your stomach that will bleed for the rest of the year.

No, the loss doesn't hurt the spectators.

Man, I'd dearly love to go to Las Vegas and gamble like a sport, if someone else would furnish the money. Great fun. But if I had to furnish my own financing, I'd think about it differently. I wouldn't throw those chips around quite as fast.

People in the stands are gambling with the coach's chips. They love to see an aggressive guy like Arnold Palmer, a swashbuckler who shoots for the flag. But it gets to a point in football, where your aggressive thinking is not practical. When you plan to swash, you buckle instead. And that's the point when you come back and play sane, conservative type of football.

We have a bunch of those fans, just like every coach, who holler, "Shoot the works, kid." I like to remind them of a story told of Paul Boesch, the former Houston wrestler who was a company commander in the European war.

> He had just taken over the outfit and didn't know the personnel when suddenly the company was pinned down in the mud under enemy fire. Paul looked around for his first sergeant.

"Sergeant Bailey," he shouted. "Sergeant Bailey, where are you?"

"Right over here, lieutenant," said the sergeant.

Paul squirmed around in the mud but still couldn't locate the sergeant. "Where? Stand up so I can see you."

"Lieutenant," growled the sergeant, "if you want to see me, **you** stand up."

That's what I feel like saying when the fans yell against the quick-kicks and the conservative defensive thinking and two-point conversion tries when a game hangs in the balance. *You* stand up. It's a little more practical here in the mud.

Casting the Roles

Primarily, we choose our players by how they play defensively. When the two-platoon arrangement was banished from collegiate rule books, most coaches turned to the defensive unit for their first teamers.

The reason is not, as some critics say, that defense is all that interests college coaches. We use defensive football as a measuring stick because it is more indicative of the rugged qualities of football.

You have to be tough to play offense, too, because there's no place for a timid person in a contact sport. But we believe defense exemplifies more the slam-bang roughness of the game. Some think it takes more talent, better timing, agility and skill to play offense. But look at it this way: A ball carrier is trying to dodge other people. His business is trying to avoid contact. That same halfback on defense is trying to get his body in collision with the other man.

There's a difference, in my opinion, between a halfback dodging people and trying to avoid contact, and the same halfback searching out violence like a hungry wolf.

The Offensive Runner Takes Less of a Beating

As a general rule, a ball carrier doesn't take a real physical beating. Not like some of the defensive men do. A ball carrier is active enough to be moving and shifting and dodging and oftentimes they're hit with a glancing tackle.

A halfback will collect more bruises on defense, in one of those wild scenes where everybody is crashing into each other in an effort to reach the ball carrier, or in an effort to keep people from him. Back in my playing days, I've been shaken many times by teammates in one of those mad traffic jams. Playing offense, I was hardly bruised at all. In my senior year, when I played practically no defense, I could have played a game every day, even though it was the Split T where quarterbacks were contacted on almost every play.

A Good Defender Plays Good Football

It may not always turn out that the better defensive players are the better football players, but it is a solid rule of thumb. Spelled out simply, it probably amounts to the fact that the more rugged type boy usually is the better defensive player. And we are inclined to favor the tougher type when we're casting our roles.

Wanted: Angry Hornets

We can talk about defensive charges of linemen, the slant, the loop, the penetrating charge and the controlled charge. And we can once again get into the business of diagramming different defenses in use today. But, frankly, I don't think all that detailed charting makes much difference.

We have used a nine-man front, with linebackers standing in like eager kibitzers. And we have used the eight-man front, the defense opposing the current Wing T formations. Through all these alignments and spacings, we have learned that the best defense is to get your lads angry and stirred up against the opposition. That's when they play good defense, regardless of what alignment they're launched from. Defense is more a test of courage and determination than of technique.

Of course, the *number one law* of defense is to meet offensive strength with defensive strength.

Draw a line splitting the middle man in the seven-man offensive line required by the rulebook, and match your opponents man-for-man in depth and width and concentration. There is a defensive philosophy that allows a coach to over-balance his defense to counteract a speed advantage of the opposing team. Also many coaches will over-shift their defense to the wide side of the field when the ball is on a hash mark.

Mostly, at Texas we just like to line up in a balanced defense, matching strength against strength, and start cracking walnuts.

When the ball changes hands, our youngsters go through something closely resembling a Chinese fire drill. Our tackles play guards on defense. One guard and the fullback are the linebackers. The center and the other guard play defensive tackles.

The theory is that we like to have our big men in the middle of the line to stop the power plays. And, of course, our tackles usually are our biggest men. Also we like to have more agility at defensive tackle and ends to pep up the pursuit.

Thus far, we've found that our particular centers play better defense in the "down" position on the defensive line, rather than in the upright position of the linebacker.

However, we're not married to this system. We'll change any time we think our personnel are more suitable to the normal pattern.

We use the strongside offensive guards as the line-backing guards. And we prefer to platoon the offensive full-back with a linebacking specialist if possible.

Putting Up a Defensive Front. The most popular college defenses of the past few years have been the eight-man front and the nine-man front. And the biggest difference in these two plans, frankly, is that one is harder to coach than the other.

The nine-man front, because of its secondary perimeter, is a tough baby to instruct. In this defense, the ends are pulled in tight and the corner linebacker stands outside the end. This corner linebacker must be taught to play three positions—on the line of scrimmage, corner back, and safety. This particular secondary perimeter rotates toward the ball, so that the corner linebacker may be charging in and busting things up if the play comes his way, or back-pedaling to a safety position if the flow of traffic is away from him.

Thus, the secondary men of the nine-man front must be taught three positions.

In the eight-man front, the ends play outside, and you use a three-man zone secondary. Your deep men divide the field into thirds and play the same territory all the time.

That's the real argument for teams switching to the eight-man front to combat the Wing T. It was so much easier to adjust to those slot backs, unbalanced lines, backs in long motion, flanker backs, spread ends, and all these strange attacks that have come up. You don't have to revolve the secondary defense. Simpler. Less confusion, which produces more aggression; the same old pattern.

There have been some adaptations of the eight-man front. Arkansas' famous "monster" defense is actually a combination of the eight-man and the nine. The front lines up like a nine-man scheme, with a roving linebacker playing to the offensive strength. The linebacker, of course, is the "monster." Actually, the Arkansas defense is overshifted on every play. Yet the Arkansas secondary is a three-deep zone affair, like the eight-man arrangement.

Bear's Commandments

In an earlier Prentice-Hall book,* Bear Bryant lists 10 commandments for his defense:

> The defense must not allow a long pass for an "easy" touchdown. Neither must it allow a long run for an "easy" score. It must not allow the opponent to score by running from within the five-yard line.
>
> The defense must not allow a kick-off return for a touchdown. It must not allow an average of more than 20 yards per kick-off return. It must intercept two passes out of every 13. It must average 20 yards per return on each interception. It must return three interceptions for touchdowns during the season.
>
> The defense must force opponents to fumble an average of 3½ times per game. The defense must recover an average of 2½ fumbles per game.

This is a wonderful ambition. We haven't established such a rigid set of requirements at Texas, but any time our defensive team wants to pass this type of resolution, the cheers will be on us.

We do try to impress the defense that it is also an offense, and that it can and will score touchdowns. During our 1962 season, the Texas defense was directly involved in 10 of the 28 scores. The defense was the scoreboard difference between a possible 7-2-1 season and the eventual 9-0-1 record. In 1961, the *Longhorn* defense was responsible for scoring or setting up 12 of the 44 scores.

The Eye-Catchers on Defense

Perhaps it's the mark of a timid man, but I would hate to point out one defensive position as more important than any other.

---

* Bryant, Paul "Bear," *Building a Championship Football Team*, Prentice-Hall, Inc., Englewood Cliffs, N. J., 1960, p. 27.

Mostly you find coaching stress placed on proper selection of linebackers. Frank Broyles insists, "We want our two best Arkansas football players at linebacker." Other coaches vow that you never see a great football team that doesn't have great linebacking.

Still, this may be a case of the chicken and the egg. Is the football team great because it has great linebacking, or is the linebacking great because it is a great football team?

In almost all defenses used today, the linebacker is the kingpin. He's in the showcase. As a footloose rover, he has a definite advantage over the "down" linemen. A defensive guard, churning down there in the bitter battle of the bulls, hasn't too many opportunities to make a tackle, compared to the linebacker. The play has to be directed fairly close to the guard before he can reach it.

But the linebacker's alignment is more luxurious. He has range and mobility and, sometimes, a free hand. In many cases, defenses are so designed that they tie up all the offensive men at the line of scrimmage.

The defensive linemen aren't expected to make a lot of tackles. They just wrap up all the blockers in the line so that no one can get through to go after the linebackers.

Alabama does a better job with this tactic than anyone else. The Alabama linemen will strip down the blockers, and their linebackers are always aggressive, mobile, and equipped with a big nose for the ball. They're turned loose as headhunters, and they have tremendous opportunities to see and be seen.

Because of these opportunities, your linebackers should be your best open field tacklers. Although I'm not saying this is the most important defensive spot.

Take the defensive guards and their ever-present danger of being trapped. You must spend hours training these two players to avoid traps. It doesn't take many traps busted through the middle to influence the scoreboard.

Therefore, defense is a team effort. The day of the

sensational individual defensive show is fading. Now the defense must be a coordinated unit.

If any one spot is more vital, it would be the safetyman. If he gets out of his zone, there's a pass down the alley for six points. He must be a steady, sure tackler. A mistake by the safety is a killer.

Ganging Up on the Ball Carrier

There has been some controversy, from time to time, over the practice of "gang tackling." Some coaches frankly teach and promote gang tackling, where six or seven defenders are in on every tackle. The objective is manifold.

First, it is demoralizing, to say the least, for a ball carrier to be banged around like a badminton bird. It wears him down physically. It lessens the possibility of his breaking away from a tackle and gaining additional yards. Most of all, he may be knocked loose from the football, and heaven hath no gift like unto a fumble.

There are such practices as "slow whistle" drills to encourage gang tackling. There are "butt drills" in which the tackler tries to drive his hat through the football in the ball carrier's arms.

We've never had any of these drills, although an intersectional opponent once accused our tacklers of holding his ball carriers upright while others butted at him like a goat.

I rather think gang tackling is a question of desire, wherein all your team is afire and individually dedicated to participation on every tackle.

There's certainly nothing wrong with tackling the ball. It's perfectly ethical for the second tackler on the scene to stick his helmet into the ball. It can result in frequent fumbles. I've never been able to understand why more coaches don't stress ball-tackling. In any class of football—high school, college or professional—ball carriers often get careless about their grip on the ball.

Figure 8: Good grief, Harper! That's no way to carry a football. Get a better grasp of the situation or you'll fumble.

It takes courage for a tackler to stick his noggin across and in front of a runner. But this is the surest way to halt transportation. We call it "going across the bow." The terminology is a holdover from our staff's stay at the University of Washington in a nautical environment. We want the defensive man's head to be shoved across in front of the ball carrier.

The reasons are obvious. If the tackler's head is behind the runner, then he's arm-tackling and there is the danger that the ball carrier may break away from the arms. If the head is in front of the runner and the defender misses the tackle, still there's a chance of catching the runner with the lower part of the body.

In intramural touch football, a flag is tied to the back of the belts. If a defender tags the flag, then the runner is "down." So when one of our tacklers sticks his head *behind* the runner, we call it "going for the flag." And that makes it a question of whether he wants to play intramural touch football, or wants to be a major college player. "Going for the flag" is not exactly a complimentary term.

Against the Public Grain

Perhaps the term "defensive football" has become a target for critics. It has come to imply a stodgy, unimaginative philosophy. Yet there is nothing unimaginative about defense. Even the professionals, with their relaxed rules and their mature, expert operators, will tell you that defense is the backbone of a winning pro team.

Likewise a "defensive team" is usually identified as one which plays conservatively, shuns gambles and risks.

A few years ago, Louisiana State had itself a crackerjack team. The *Tigers* were unbeaten and untied in 19 games and the bayou people wanted them cast in bronze.

The *Tigers* and their coach, Paul Dietzel, took their national No. 1 rating up to Knoxville for a go at Tennessee. The *Vols* were in front 14-7, with most of the last quarter left on the clock. LSU scored to narrow the gap to 14-13,

Figure 9: This *Razorback* tackler, with only his arm barring Texas fullback Ray Poage, may lose his man. The head goes first in front of the target to secure the tackle.

with the option of trying the two-point conversion run or pass, or settling for the much surer one-point place-kick.

Coach Dietzel scorned the one-point kick. ("We didn't come to Knoxville to play for a tie," he said later.) The *Tigers* went for broke, sending their supreme hero, Billy Cannon, smacking into the line after those precious three yards. The play failed by one yard. LSU was unable to score again; the LSU winning streak was broken.

All around the country, the *Tigers* were applauded for their courage. But the people who were doing the clapping were cheering a gamble with the other fellow's chips. A poll of the nation's coaches probably would have disagreed with the decision to try for two points, especially with ample time left in the game to score again. This, apparently, was an ill-chosen moment for a gamble.

Which was exactly how the Irishman felt on his death bed when the priest called on him to renounce the devil and all his works.

"I beg to differ, Father," said Mike. "This is no time for me to be making enemies."

I wish the public would remember that these are our chips we're playing with. Coaches might be more inclined to play the hell-for-leather games if their bread and butter weren't at stake. But it is, and good solid defense has always been the backbone of successful college records. Call it unimaginative if you will. I think *practical* is a better word.

chapter seven

Men and Boys Separate at the Goal Line

The 50-yard-line ticket is a wonderful prestige instrument. It has become a magnificent status symbol in America.

If you have a couple tickets squarely in the middle for The Big Game, you can stick them in your breast pocket and suddenly you are Mr. Big. Some smarty always will grab them from your pocket and inspect the location. Watch his eyebrows.

"Got a couple on the fifty for tomorrow's game," you say modestly to the boys in the office, in much the same tone as you would announce your election as president of General Motors.

You stalk to the stadium, make a late arrival at your 50-yard-line seats so people may notice your exalted station in life. You have a splendid view of that vast expanse of green turf in front of the benches and the band will salute you at halftime. But you're considerably removed from the most important territory in the confines, the brutal No Man's Land of the goal line.

Football games are decided from the 20-yard-line on in. All that other running and panting out in the middle of the field is just entertaining spectators and wearing out grass.

Mainly, football consists of two basic operations: taking the ball off your own goal, and taking it in those final 10 yards toward the other goal line. All that other business is just simply the promotion of bigger and better ticket sales.

It's how well you play defense on the goal line that separates the champions from the people who just play football for lack of something else to do.

Champions Make Goal Line Stands

The goal line is where the moment of truth comes and it's no place for a timid person. Both teams are boxed into a limited area, there in the final 10 yards of play. You don't play pass defense. Your secondary can move up to the front trenches. That good old byword, pursuit, is no good here. Your linemen can't be hitting and pursuing. It doesn't help you to give ground and cut off the ball carrier five yards deep, because by then the bands will be playing, the cannon will be firing, and several thousand spectators will be rubbing frankfurter mustard into the shoulders of people immediately to their right.

Down there in that wild dogfight, it's a slash-bang, penetrating, aggressive type of defense. You can play stubborn defense in the middle of the field, give ground grudgingly, and hope for an opponent's mistake. But on your own front porch finesse takes a holiday.

As a matter of fact, it is not defense at all. The successful goal line defense is one that thinks *offensively*. The defense must attack. I'll have nothing of waiting back; waiting to see where the ball is going and then going to it. You must be just as aggressive-minded as the offense is against you. You are not the defender. You must think offensively.

Fix Bayonets and Charge

There are several sets of mechanics for goal line defenses. Here again, the simpler, the better. If ever a lad doesn't have a chance to think, it's on the goal line where the speed is so magnified by the occasion.

Generally, the defensive ends must seal off the inside, charging at a 45-degree angle. Tackles should crack inside or through the offensive tackles, pinching toward the middle. Guards are usually directed at the center's shoulders. Regular linebackers jam plays between the tackles, and the drawn-up secondary has the wide responsibilities.

Linemen drop to all four points with chins touching the tall grass and their explosions must be low and pinching toward the middle jam. An ideally successful goal line defensive charge would find all linemen shoulder to shoulder in a cupped arc, one yard across the line of scrimmage, with fire spewing from each nostril. This is nice to dream about.

Goal Line Is a Test for All

Any team in the country is going to be put to this goal line test. There's no way a team can go through a season and keep opponents off its goal line. They will intercept a pass, block a punt, cover a fumble, turn a double somersault, land on their eyebrows and catch a freak pass—somehow they're going to reach your goal line.

And this is true in almost every game. You just can't keep people from your end of the field. Today's teams are too evenly matched.

A squad must accept this grim fact. We go into every game admitting that the other outfit is going to knock on our front door. We must decide before the game how tough we will become over their trespassing. Each Saturday morning before a game, our coaching staff keeps hammering away at this point. It takes a constant selling job by the coaches.

First, goal line defenses are about 50 percent confidence. You must believe your goal line defense is the best in the land.

Your players must believe that *they* have the advantage when the ball is inside their own 10-yard line, because it eliminates much of the offense's choice of operation. Your players have less territory to cover, so the advantage is *theirs*.

When your opponents reach the 10, heaven forbid, your young men should assume a positive attitude. *Okay,* you guys, you've had the advantage up to now. But now it's our turn. We're all going to get together here on this little spot of ground and see who's boss.

If a defensive team truly believes the advantage belongs to it, then that's half the battle, because half of goal line defense is confidence. If your team *thinks* the opposing eleven can't score, it will probably be right.

Proof Positive in the Record Books

Every team with a winning record has a proud history of goal line defenses. The 1950 Kentucky team, *Sugar Bowl* champions with a 10-1 season record, had the amazing history of 19 successful repulses from its own three-yard line.

In our first six years at Texas, the *Longhorn* goal line defense was successful 28 times inside the 10-yard line.

And in 11 games where that defense stood up, the outcome was decided by less than one touchdown. Three of them were ties and the other eight were Texas wins. In other words, goal line stands actually won eight games for us and turned three others into ties.

During that stretch, Texas had a won-lost-tied record of 48-14-3. Take away those goal line stands and the record could easily have been 40-25. A difference between a .615 batting average and a .762.

I mentioned earlier the Texas-Texas A&M game of 1959, when the *Aggies* were faced with a short yardage situation 11 times during the game and were successful in making the necessary space on 10 occasions. The other occasion was on the Texas one-yard line, and that decided the 20-17 game.

And psychological lifts? In 1961, we were unbeaten coming into the SMU game (six wins) and the *Mustangs* proceeded to give us a holy fit. It was 0-0 at halftime.

However, in the second quarter, SMU had put together a drive and suddenly we were in misery up to our

Figure 10: Here is goal line defense at its best. Texas linebacker Pat Culpepper (31) stops SMU's John Ed Clarke on the *Longhorns'* 2-yard line. This was a big second quarter play in the 1961 game that was 0-0 at the half. Texas exploded in the second half for a 27-0 win.

necks. The *Methodists* were on our six-yard line with four downs to score.

Then the old goal line adrenalin started pumping and our linebackers, Pat Culpepper and Johnny Treadwell, became part buffalo and part volcano. SMU was stopped on four downs and from the Texas player celebration, you would have thought we had just won the World Series on four successive no-hitters. It gave the team a tremendous lift. Shortly after the half, Saxton whipped off an 80-yard scoring run and we came in a four-touchdown winner.

Even more dramatic was a goal line stand in 1962, when we met Arkansas in the fifth game of the season. Both teams were unbeaten and the experts were predicting the conference champion would come out of this game. (As indeed it did.)

It was a fierce game. Arkansas had a 3-0 lead in the third quarter and the *Porkers* were just about to increase it out of range. From the one-yard line, on third down, the big Arkansas fullback, Danny Brabham, tore into the middle. He dived high over the line and was met in mid-air by Culpepper, with Treadwell only a split-second behind. The ball bounced loose, Texas recovered, a backbreaking touchdown was saved. And our team was so invigorated by this experience that we were able to march 85 yards in the last quarter to win the crucial game, 7-3. It was the only regular season game Arkansas lost. And it was, other than a tie with Rice, our closest game in an unbeaten season.

Goal Lines Breed Fanaticism

When you are faced with a goal line defense, that's when you'll find out who the real tough football players are. Sometimes you're surprised at their identity, such as the ones who turn fanatical and play a little bit better than it's possible for someone of their physical talents.

But you never know the extent of a boy's determination until he meets this separation point on the field.

Here again is goal line defense at its finest. Texas linebackers Johnny Treadwell (60) and Pat Culpepper (31) meet Arkansas' Danny Brabham on the 1-yard line and jar the ball loose for a Texas recovery. This was the most important single play in Texas' 7-3 victory over Arkansas in a battle of unbeaten teams which decided the 1962 Southwest Conference title.

One of our Southern coaches likes to tell his squad the story about the part-time "preacher" who was sent, many years ago, to a tough prison.

> The first day, the warden called him in. "We assign each prisoner a job and a goal each day," he said. "You report to the cotton-picking gang. And we want you to pick 150 pounds today. Can you do it?"
>
> "Yassuh," the prisoner grinned, "the good Lawd willing, I can."
>
> But he picked only 125 pounds, so the next morning he was called before the warden again.
>
> "Maybe you didn't understand me," said the official. "We expect you to meet that goal. Now today, your goal goes up. It's 175 pounds. Can you do it?"
>
> "The good Lawd willing, I can," said the prisoner again.
>
> Again he fell short by 25 pounds. After several days of this shortcoming and this dependency on spiritual aid, the prisoner was taken off and given a stern taste of the whip. It made a definite impression on him.
>
> The following morning, the warden said, "Well, now you see we mean business. Your goal today is 250 pounds. Can you get it?"
>
> "Warden, I'll tell you one thing," said the prisoner, "if that blankity-blank cotton is out there, I'll get it!"

That's the way it is with goal line defense and winning teams. You not only can—you must.

chapter eight

There is no part of football that's kicked around as much as the kicking part.

First, fans seem to shower disrespect on a team that puts heavy stress on punting. And if a team uses the quick kick, they'll scream, "Give-up football!" until they're as purple as eggplants. Second, youngsters don't practice "vacant lot" kicking nearly as much as they used to, and not nearly as much as they should. Third, coaches are even neglectful in teaching certain aspects of kicking. And yet it is just about the heart of the entire game; and maybe the liver also.

In practically all close football games, some part of the kicking game will be the deciding factor: a long punt out of bounds on the three-yard line; perhaps; a fumbled catch by the safety man; a bad snap by the center on a kick-

Kick:

A Four-Letter Word

ing down; a blocked punt; a field goal, or a blocked try.

You'll have a hard time convincing the spectators or the pressboxers of it, but kicking yardage is just as influential on the scoreboard as the yards gained rushing or passing.

Evaluating the Kicking Game

We judge our Texas kicking game by its net worth. Take a particular game and say that we kicked eight times for a total of 320 yards and the other team returned those punts for a total of 10. This gives us a net of 310 yards.

Our opposition kicked six times for 240 yards and we returned punts for a total of 20 yards. Okay, they have a net total of 220 yards against our 310 yards.

That 90 yards advantage is just as valuable as 90 yards of rushing or passing. This is concealed yardage. It never shows up in a statistical report. Statistics are supposed to tell the story of ball movement up and down the field, but the punting factor gets slighted in the narrative.

Critics will hand you that "give-up football" business when you quick-kick or punt the ball on an early down. But if you get the darn thing down at the other end of the field, it's just as effective as if you pushed down there on a long, punishing drive and stalled on downs.

Kicking Is a Weapon, Not a Shield. Fans may not consider it a weapon, but if they were in a coach's shoes when the opposition punts dead inside the 15-yard line, they'd feel it like a lump in the mattress. The opposition has just used a weapon to cut your offense in half.

The change in the rules (allowing the kicking team to kill the ball inside the 10-yard line) puts even more stress on the punt. There is more punting, probably more early-down punting, and the advantage is with the attacking team, as it should be.

Some critics greeted the rule change with hoots and moans. Wrote one columnist:

> If there is anything less inspiring than three-yards-and-a-cloud-of-dust rushing game, it is a punting duel.

Maybe so, but most coaches consider punting an art, and a most important weapon. Of course, coaches are mostly concerned with trying to win ball games, rather than set a new record for raising chill bumps.

Texas' Staff's Philosophy on Kicking

Our coaching staff has been influenced largely by the kicking philosophy and techniques of the Tennessee clan, people like Bobby Dodd, Bowden Wyatt, and Bob Woodruff. Goodness knows, no coach ever placed more stress on kicking than Gen. Bob Neyland, patriarch of that particular tribe. The general loved to have a strong-legged youngster who could keep the opponents backed against the cliff edge all afternoon, waiting for that inevitable mistake.

In breaking down the Texas game films, we find approximately *one-fourth* of the footage is taken up by various facets of the kicking department. This includes punts, kickoffs, returns, extra points, field goals, and fake kicks.

Therefore, we consider kicking one-fourth of the game. Offense and defense equally absorb the other three-fourths.

With this as a standard, we try to spend one-fourth of our practice time talking or working on kicking. If you don't balance the practice time in proportion to the actual game time on different departments, then you're wasting valuable minutes somewhere.

Our films, as mentioned before, are cut and spliced into three reels—the offensive plays, the defensive plays, the kicking game. We show the kicking films on Wednesday or Thursday, but, of course, we spend time on kicks every day.

Maybe it's because I was always so crazy about punting, but I'm a bit disappointed in the college kickers of today. There wasn't a summer that I didn't practice kicking five days a week. I'd run down somebody to help chase the ball, or if no one was available, I'd hotfoot it myself. After September drills started, many's the time I'd stay late and ask somebody to set out a plate at the training table in case the kitchen closed before I got there. I did it because I thoroughly enjoyed it.

I just don't believe kids enjoy it as much today. Some people will argue that kicking is a fading art because youngsters' legs aren't as strong as they once were. Too many automobiles and not enough walking. If this be true, why is it that boys are running faster than ever and jumping higher and longer? It's not the leg strength that's missing, it's the interest.

And this is a mystery. A good punter always has himself a job. He might be ill-fitted for other departments of the game, but if he can make that ball behave with his foot, then people will seek him out, bearing gifts.

Never Mind the Technique

Punting a football is an awkward business at most. You must balance on one leg and boot an elongated spheroid that's not really built for booting.

There are attempts to place good punters under a magnifying glass and draw up a rigid set of rules for everybody. Some coaches want the ball held just so, with the middle finger of the right hand resting along the bottom seam, the ball dropped from waist high, 18 inches in front of the kicking hip.

But it's awfully easy to overcoach a punter. If he does the job adequately, we are loath to change his kicking technique.

There also is a fine science of timing used by many coaches. They'll take their stop-watches to the practice field and establish split-second standards.

From the spread punt formation, they say, the center should be able to snap the ball 13 yards to the punter in six-tenths of a second. (Kicking from the spread punt, the very first requirement is a center who can snap the ball 13 yards with accuracy. If you don't have this, forget it.)

Then, the clock-watchers want the punter to get the ball away in 1.3 seconds. They want the punt to hang in the air for another four seconds. They figure the linemen will spend one second on their blocks and then will have 4.9 seconds to rush downfield and clobber the man catching the ball.

It would be real nice if you could have all those things, just as it would be handy if your ends were 6-4 and fast, and your tackles were agile 250-pounders, and your father the president of A.T.&T.

The Stop-watch Is a Reminder. But we don't go into it quite this scientifically. Oh, we put the stop-watch to them, all right. Backfield coach Bill Ellington hangs the

Figure 12: Quite a feat! This put a real sock into our offense in the 1962 Texas-Oklahoma game. Tony Crosby delivered a stockinged field goal that defeated Oklahoma 9-6. A pointed lesson to leave an effective kicking style alone.

thing around his neck and works with the punters. But to be absolutely truthful about it, the reason for the stop watch is to impress the center and the kicker that we're timing them and to be conscious of getting the kick off as quickly as possible. In other words, if they're trying as hard as they can, a stop watch is not going to make them kick any faster. It does represent a symbol, or a reminder, that Jack must be nimble and Jack must be quick, or Jack may eat pigskin for lunch.

I never have really sat down and studied it, but if the entire kicking operation takes only two seconds, you should be safe enough.

Distance Kicking—Past and Present

Sometimes, from the tight punt formation of yesteryear, there were instances of a punter outkicking his coverage. His punt would sail along and beautifully down the field, while his protecting linemen spent at least two seconds on their blocks. This gave the safetymen blessed time to catch the ball, consult their road maps and start off on their travels.

Nowadays, with the spread formation in vogue, there isn't much danger of *over*-kicking. There is the danger, however, of a punter keeping the ball too low.

After all, we're not too interested in the length of the punt. We want to see the figures after the safetyman has finished his jumping around. We're interested in the *net* yardage after the return is subtracted. This makes the punt a teamwork affair, between the kicker and his teammates who are covering.

After the rule change allowing a punted ball to be killed inside the 10-yard line, the "punch" kick became popular, a little hit-and-roll punt that squirms and skips around and gives the kicking team a chance to kill it close to the goal line. You don't see punters standing back, throwing out their chests, striding big and kicking for the flag anymore.

The Punter's Check-list

Confucius, or some coach of his day, has said that there have been many great kickers, but very few great punters.

Even in practice, a punter should never put foot to the ball without doing some quick thinking. The brain is just as important as the foot.

The punter should have a check-list that runs through his dome. The score, the time of the game, the weather, wind, the field position, the number and position of safety-men, the down. (Certainly the down. There is absolutely no excuse for having an early-down kick blocked).

He should notice if the defense is assembling at any specific point. Is the rush on? Will they try to concentrate rushers and block this kick, or will they concentrate on the return? And he must always alert himself to the possibilities of a bad snap. It should never take him by surprise.

We had a kicker at Texas named Walter Fondren who was a marvel with his head as well as his foot. He was extremely cool and he could read a defense like the big letters on an eye chart.

It's not hard to tell when the defense will try to block this punt. They're all jammed in there and trembling with eagerness, and you know you can't waste any time getting the ball away.

Fondren could sense when the defense was concentrating on the return. He'd stand and hold the ball and look calmly downfield, giving his teammates a chance to invade the territory. Then, when a couple of defenders would notice him standing back there and start their rush, he'd kick it just before they reached him. I've never seen his equal at this technique. He could kick quickly, with his knee drawn up. He could kick on the run if necessary. Or he could step out big and boom it down there. Fondren enjoyed kicking; he was an exception.

Of course, not all kickers can have this talent. Some of them have a horrible time just getting the ball on their foot. They don't have time to stand around looking at the defense, seeing if they will rush or not.

Another thing. Now, when kickers do practice punting on their own, they all want to kick with the wind behind them, so they can see that ball sail way down the pasture. You can easily get a false impression of your own kicking, if there's any wind stirring. A better test is to kick into the wind. When it's blowing against you, kicking is just like golf. That's when you have to sock the ball true.

The Boomerang of Blocked Kicks

Don Pierce, the part-time philosopher and full-time publicity man at the University of Kansas, says there are two statements a coach always makes when he moves into a new job.

- "I'm sure gonna change these uniforms."
- "I haven't had a punt blocked in four years."

Of course, there are not as many blocked punts now that the spread formation is in vogue. Mostly, it will be a case of a bad snap from center. Some people claim that 98 percent of blocked punts are the center's fault. But the punter may be at fault. He may take too long, or he may step out of his protection pocket. James Saxton had this fault; he stepped to his right as he punted, leaving the protective cup in front of him and kicking right into the defensive charge.

Really, there's not much excuse for a blocked punt. With the kicker 13 yards back, and a true snap from center, no rusher should get into the vital zone. The protection is set up so that rushers have to go the longest distance from their starting point to get into the area right in front of the kicker. Under normal protection, no rusher blocks a kick running in a straight line. The blockers make the rusher run around them, and then it's impossible for him to block the kick.

Figure 13: Texas' Olen Underwood (69), after skirting the defense, rushes down Nightmare Alley to pressure Baylor's Mike Broyles (82). Underwood won't make it to the vital zone, but such determination often rattles the punter.

Use the Spread Punt Formation

You can use the spread punt formation from anywhere except inside your own three-yard line. The reason, of course, is that the punter must have 13 yards of freedom. Any time we're backed up on our goal, we'll try to nudge that ball at least out to the three, so we can use the spread formation. It's that important. Even on the one- or two-yard lines, we'll use a tightened down spread.

But here again, the punter must be thinking. He must realize that he has less than 13 yards of grace. The blockers must be thinking. They must hold their block an instant longer. Certainly, the "personal protector" blocker must realize the cramped distance.

This cost us a game one time at Washington. We were playing UCLA and we were leading in the game. UCLA had a great kicker in Kirk Wilson. He led the nation in 1956. He pumped a long kick downfield that died on our one-foot line. It was a rainy day. We had a lead and it was very muddy, so we decided to kick on first down. Our up-back forgot the position on the field and unconsciously assumed our punter had a full 13 yards to use. He backed into the kicker and blocked our own punt and it lost the game for us.

The boy should have realized that the kicker couldn't get a full 13 yards deep. But I also should have had sense enough to work on that particular situation beforehand. As a coach, I simply had neglected to review that possibility.

You can bet your cookie jar there's not a week goes by nowadays that we don't practice that same situation. We put the ball on our one-yard line and practice punt protection. We do this on Thursdays. The situation may never come up. It might be a season or two seasons before we have to kick from that position. But when it arrives, I want to make sure we can kick the ball and not have some sleepy guy stick his big backside in the way.

Punt Practice

In punt practice, I think teams should always kick into the other guy's goal, or kick away from their own. Punt practice in the middle of the field is wasted time. If you can handle the punt situations on your own front porch or be able to kick it into the other fellow's front porch, then you can kick anywhere.

Also, we like our centers to make deliberate bad snaps during punting drils. A kicker must always be alert for these rascals. If all the practice snaps are perfect, a bad snap during the game may take him completely by surprise and produce home-made tragedy.

It would be ideal if the squad could square off and practice punting under scrimmage pressure every day. It would be helpful for the punters and field goal kickers to have to think under actual combat conditions every time they kicked the ball. But we don't follow through on this, mainly because we don't like to use contact work every day.

The Goldplated Quick-Kick

Some fans go into a state of shock when you mention quick-kick. A coach probably hears more criticism about this particular facet of the college game than any other.

But we must defend the fort, bloody and stubborn, and say that the quick-kick is a tremendous offensive weapon. I don't believe the 1957 Texas team would have survived the season without Walter Fondren's quick-kicking. As it was, we had a fairly respectable 6-3-1 season. This doesn't include the *Sugar Bowl* game against Mississippi, a result which happily escapes me at the moment.

Here again, there are differences of opinion on kicking technique. Most coaches prefer the "sidewinding kick," which has been in fashion for a few years.

From the T Formation, the kicker may receive the ball on a direct snap, through the quarterback's legs, or he may take a pitch-back from the quarterback. In any case, the sidewinder kicker turns to face the sideline. He swings his kicking foot in a looping arc, trying to catch the tail end of the ball on his right arch. Then he legswings across his body toward the goal line in his follow-through. This action gives the ball an end-over-end punch that carries the ball low and sends it bouncing toward the goal line once it hits ground.

We don't insist on that form. Any way the kicker wants to boot it is all right, as long as he gets it away in a hurry, gets it to hit and roll. Saxton just used his regular punting form and speeded up his action. We've used the quick-kick from a simple double wing formation, jumping out of the huddle quickly, snapping the ball to the tailback and hoping to get the whole operation finished before the defense can recover. Also, we've used the sidewinder kick from the T Formation, where the quarterback pitches the ball back to a halfback and he starts to his right as if a sweep is in progress. The line fires ahead as if it were a play. Then the kicker stops and sideswipes the ball downfield.

From the double wing formation, our line simply holds fast, for the kicker lines up six or seven yards deep. On most quick-kick blocking, coaches prefer that their lines try to move the defenders back a yard. In other words, advance the line of scrimmage ahead one step, to give the kicker room.

We've always made use of the quick-kick until the Flip-Flop offense seemed to move the ball so well that we had little occasion for it. We used it only twice during the 1961 season. But with the type of offense we had before, the "three-yards-and-a-cloud-of-dust," we felt our chances of putting the ball in play 12 or 15 times on a scoring drive were practically nil.

The time will come, I'm sure, when we'll again make frequent use of the quick-kick. A man needs all the weapons he can find.

Pigskin Prestidigitation

Because kicking is such an important part of football, it definitely lends itself to fakery. Fake punts, fake field goals, fake quick-kicks, on-side kickoffs. Many of these plays take a powerful lot of stomach to use, because they must be called on a sure kicking down when failure means death by torture.

I'll never forget preparing for the *Cotton Bowl* game of 1959, against that powerful Syracuse outfit of Ernie Davis, Art Baker and friends. We dreamed up a bit of witchcraft and spent long hours on it.

Bobby Lackey was our quarterback and punter. He was a big lad with sure baseball hands. We would come out of the huddle into spread punt formation, with Lackey stationed 13 yards deep. Our center, Jerry Muennink, would snap the ball deliberately to Lackey's right, trying to make it hit the ground even with Lackey and bounce past him. Lackey would turn and chase the ball, while the defensive team grew wild in its eagerness to get back there and pounce on Lackey or the ball or both. But remember that Lackey has a 13-yard head start on them.

Our linemen were supposed to bump the rushers briefly and then let them loose to chase Lackey. Lackey, meanwhile, could easily run the ball down, straighten up and throw a simple screen pass.

The defensive linemen get so excited at seeing the ball flop around back there, they forget about all responsibilities. Lackey, with his 13-yard margin of grace, had ample time to fetch the ball and throw to a back huddled behind the offensive lineman, according to our strategy.

We worked and worked on this scheme in secret practice until we were convinced it was a safe play.

Lackey called it twice in the first half of the Syracuse game. One time the ball bounced up and hit him in the chest and he just managed to capture it and get it away—into the ground. The other time, it was completed beautifully to a Texas lineman who made an admirable, although highly illegal, catch. Still the fake bad snap was so smooth, that few people realized it was a deliberate thing. Muennink was injured and didn't play the second half, but the press box thought I had taken him out because he made two bad snaps on fourth down punts.

Oklahoma pulled a nifty fake quick-kick against Texas several years ago. The *Sooners* used their fullback as the quick-kicker and the ball was snapped directly from the center, through the quarterback's legs.

On this particular play (with Oklahoma using the non-rhythmic starting count), the fullback made a quick step backward with his left foot, as if he were starting his rocker step. It looked, for all the world, as if the fullback had forgotten the snap signal and had anticipated the ball too early and given the play away. The Texas secondary turned and fled backward, the ends trembled with eagerness to crash inside and block the quick-kick.

When the ball was finally snapped, the fullback proceeded with his quick-kick motion, handing the ball off behind his back to Tommy McDonald in the old Statue of Liberty play. McDonald dashed about 45 yards before the Texas defenders recovered.

Texas was successful with the simple fake quick-kick during Saxton's last two years. We would rush out of the huddle into the double wing formation, which we never used except for quick-kicking. The ball would be snapped back to Saxton and he simply swept outside the ends, who usually are looking for the quick-kick and come barrelling inside to the tiny kicking zone, forgetting about their containment responsibilities. Saxton had enough speed to cut around the crashing ends before they could recover.

The on-side kickoff is an old favorite, where the kicker nudges the ball with the side of his foot, trying to get it 10 yards down the field so the kicking team can legally recover it.

Someone asked me recently, "If the on-side kickoff is such a good play when a team is behind in the last few minutes, why isn't it a good play early in the game?"

The answer was: It *is* a good play any time, if we coaches just had enough guts to pull it.

Mostly the on-side kickoff is used as a desperation measure, when everybody in the stadium is expecting it. Still, it's often successful.

Kicking Time Can Be Loafing Time

I don't know why it is, but kick coverage is the time when the average college football player will think, "let George do it." He thinks, well, there are nine other guys covering this kick, and somebody will get down there and make the tackle.

Where this becomes dangerous is when four or five boys have that thought at the same time on a hot afternoon when they're winded. And that's when you get those punt returns against you that break your spine.

For that reason, we try to preach that covering kicks is football's biggest test of courage.

We have discovered this solid fact: *If a team is inclined to loaf at all, it will loaf on punt coverage.*

Some teams won't loaf at all. But if one has the faintest tendency to take it easy, this is when it will be.

So our sermon is this: Here is our chance to get the advantage over the other side, maybe the only advantage we'll have in the entire 60 minutes of play. Here is one area of the game in which hustle may pay off for us. We try to make it a competitive thing. We keep the punt returns posted, both ours and the opponent's, each week.

Punt Coverage Techniques

Techniques of punt coverage are simple, once you have convinced the players not to let "George" do it.

From the spread punt formation, the coverage fans out to cover the field and then gradually pinches in. The first man to reach the safetyman takes a murderous shot at him. He doesn't slow up, he storms in there chest high. This makes the safetyman do one of two things. He's not going to come straight at that onrushing first man. He must stop, or he must fake to one side or the other. The first man's aggressive try at a tackle will either make connections, or it will force the safetyman to stop and start over. By the time he's started off again, that's when we want the hungry pack to hit.

We don't want our ends to be the first men down. They are the containing men, guarding the outside. They mustn't be circled by the safetyman, but must close in gradually on the flanks of the pack.

When the lineman leaves his blocking post and heads downfield after the punt, he must really crank it up until he gets eight yards from the receiver. Then he must slow down, get his balance and get into a "hitting position" with his feet solidly under him. Then, after the hatchet man has forced the safetyman to stop and start anew, the pinchers move in, with full control of their speed. Every man has a responsibility on punt coverage, either containing on the outside by the ends, being the first man downfield with a full-throttle collision effort, or filling in the "cup" perimeter that closes in on the poor safetyman.

Jack Collins did our kicking one year and he wasn't a really gifted punter, not one who could wait for the rushers or kick to a certain spot. He just hauled off and booted the ball the best way he could. But we had good results because no one returned a kick.

Jack's punt return-avoidance figures were as good as Fondren's in 1957, because our coverage was so improved. In 1957, the opposition averaged 1.67 yards returning Fondren's kicks. In 1961, opponents averaged 1.9 returning. You just don't improve on those figures.

The Payoff Fumble

There is another big incentive to prevent that loafing on punt coverage. A downrushing tackler is not only going down to crash into the safetyman. He's running down there to recover that fumble. He's not furnished with a written guarantee that the safetyman is going to catch the ball. He's not sure and the safetyman's darn sure not positive. Our heroes must never relax, even if the safety signals for a fair catch, because that fumble is apt as not to be up for grabs.

The average player may huff and puff downfield a couple times and keep the fumble in mind. Then it becomes a chore and his feet hurt, and it's awfully hot. On perhaps 15 occasions the safetyman makes clean catches. Also, maybe the 16th time the ball will get away from him and it will mean the ball game.

Here's some examples:

- In 1957, George Blanch recovered a fumbled punt that turned the Texas tide against Georgia. That same year, he hounded an Arkansas safetyman who fumbled a fair catch and promptly led to a field goal.
- In 1958, the same Texas back covered another fumbled punt by Georgia that led to a score. Guard Mike Wells in the same game did likewise. (Three recovered fumbled punts in two years were the only difference between Texas and Georgia.)
- In 1959, Bill Laughlin recovered a fumbled catch by the Arkansas safetyman, leading to a touchdown and a 14-13 Texas victory.
- In 1960, Laughlin and Don Talbert recovered two against Maryland, one leading to a touchdown on the following play. The same season, Mike Cotten and James Saxton pounced on two more.

In those four years, Texas recovered nine fumbled punts; five led directly to *Longhorn* scores.

And some people call it luck when you recover a fumble by the safetyman. That's what we mean by saying, "Luck is what happens when preparation meets with opportunity." You went down under the punt to recover that fumble in the first place. If not this time, next time.

The Rule Book Is Required Reading

Walk into any college locker room and ask this question: "What if a punt hits in the end zone, and then bounces back out into the field of play? How is it played?" You'll get the dangdest set of answers. It's almost a cinch bet, they won't be in unison.

There is more indecision, more confusion in the kicking game than in any other part of football. And mostly it is the coaches' fault. Most of us simply do not teach the rules governing various kicking situations.

What if a safetyman signals for a fair catch, and one of his teammates catches the ball and runs with it? This happened to us in a conference game, and the official allowed the gain, although our players protested bitterly. They were right; he was wrong. Fortunately, it didn't affect the game's outcome.

In the 1957 Texas-Arkansas game, the *Longhorns* kicked into a strong wind. The Arkansas safetyman signaled for a fair catch. The ball struck a wind current and started to fall considerably short of the safetyman. But since he had signaled for a fair catch, he *thought* he *had* to catch the ball. He made a mad dive for it, it bounced off his shoulder pads, Monte Lee recovered it for Texas, and Fred Bednarski kicked a field goal a few plays afterward. The Arkansas boy just didn't know the rules. He didn't know he didn't *have* to try to catch the ball, just because he signaled fair catch.

Another example: At a Georgia Tech-Miami game a few years ago, I saw Miami punt to a double *Tech* safety. One safety signaled for a fair catch. The Miami tacklers relaxed. But this particular safety didn't touch the ball. It hit the ground, bounced, the other safety scooped it up on the run and whipped right by the relaxed defenders for a touchdown run that won a 7-0 game.

In the TCU-Air Force game in the *Cotton Bowl* several years ago, I saw two extreme examples. Air Force punted to the *Frogs* and the kick went into the end zone. The ball was curling around in its bounces, however, and it looked as if it might bounce back on the field of play. The TCU safetyman quickly and smartly, killed the ball in the end zone. If it had bounced onto the field, of course, it would be in play where the ball stopped dead. Instead, TCU got the ball on its own 20.

On another occasion, however, TCU was kicking into deep Air Force territory and the ball looked as if it might have a slim chance of rolling into the end zone. So a TCU tackle killed it on the one. Under rules then, the ball came out to the 20. He had nothing to gain by killing it. He didn't know the rules. His safetyman did.

How about a partially-blocked punt that goes beyond the line of scrimmage? How many players can give you the ruling on that? In the Texas-TCU game of 1960, a TCU player partially blocked Saxton's kick deep in our territory. It went high in the air, across the line of scrimmage. A TCU guard almost broke his neck leaping high in the air to catch it. He thought it was a free ball, when, of course, it wasn't. He fumbled his desperate grab, and Saxton recovered, to give us a new set of downs. It was a vital play in a game that went to Texas, 3-2.

College players simply are not well-versed in the rule book concerning the kicking game. Here again, we try to convince the players that they must know the rules under all situations. We drill the squad over and over on those rules. It may be one of those slight advantages that some day, this season, next season, some Saturday, might win us a ball game. Besides, it gives the players a happy lift when one of those tricky kick situations comes up and they know the rules on it.

There is simply no end to the possibilities of a good sound kicking game as an offensive weapon, or the importance of all-out coverage of kicks.

Figure 14: Texas A&M's Travis Reagan double-thinks on this Texas punt and wisely declines to accept it on his own 1-yard line. A swarm of Texas defenders kills the ball on the *Aggie* five rather than have it squirt into the end zone. Everyone knew the rules on this play.

chapter nine

Field Position Football

Coaches aren't known for their benevolent nature, but it's said that it is far more blessed to give than to receive, and I'd like to give something away.

Twice a game, I would like to donate possession of the ball to the other team.

Instead of a kickoff at the beginning of each half, let the other team have the ball on its 20-yard line.

Trouble on Their Doorstep

Eliminate the coin flip, as far as we're concerned. You may have the ball and start your chugging away, down deep in your own territory. Your offensive repertoire is severely limited, and you must be careful you don't fumble, or get a pass intercepted, or botch a handoff, or get a bad snap from center on your punting down. If you do, that's where our blessed generosity will pay off.

We'd rather you take the ball on your own 20, than for us to have possession on our own 20.

Almost all college coaches subscribe to this theory, except a few proponents of the pro-type passing offense. In my particular case, I preach Field Position so much that I'm often kidded about it.

Morris Frank, the celebrated Houston toastmaster, once presided at a dinner for Southwest Conference coaches. As Morris introduced each one, the coach would stand and say a few words about the prospects for his season. I was unable to attend, but Morris filled in for me.

"We won't miss him," Morris said. "I'll tell you, for Royal, that the Texas' success depends upon field posi-

tion." He was just about right, too, whether kidding or not.

Most of the time, unless you have poor *Field Position*, you won't be scored on. Oh, of course, there will be that occasional 80-yard touchdown run or the long completed pass when a defender gets caught out of position. But those are the exceptions for a sound defensive club.

On the other hand, how many 80-yard scoring drives do you see? The odds are stacked against a team driving 80 yards without some sort of mishap—a penalty, a fumble, a busted signal, a bad snap. Against Arkansas, in our most important game of 1962, the Texas team drove 85 yards in the last quarter for the winning touchdown, twice making vital four-down yardage. But the odds against this move were about comparable to those for winning the Irish Sweepstakes.

If our opponents have the ball on their 20, we believe *we* have a better chance of scoring than they do. We feel *we're* on *offense*. We're just 20 yards from a touchdown and they're looking at 80 yards of tough grass.

The Offense Can Be Stopped by Chance

Ordinarily an offensive team will stop itself about 65 percent of the time, either by a fumble, a penalty, a missed signal, or some similar tragedy.

So, unless we're behind in the game and the clock is running out, any time our opponents want the ball behind their 20, we'll even giftwrap it. That's *Field Position football* and the percentages are heavily in its favor.

Here again, some people will brand it "give-up football," when you kick on an early down, or quick-kick to get the ball deep into the other guy's territory. The critics say this theory shows a lack of confidence in your own offense. But most coaches don't think so, and they're the ones who study the percentages. We believe it's bold, aggressive football to put the pressure on the other fellow right there on his own front porch. The percentages say he'll foul up one way or the other.

The Late-in-the-Game Quick-Kick

I've even heard of one major college coach who quick-kicked when he was one point behind and less than a minute to play! It so happened that the receiving team fumbled the ball, and the fortunate fellow recovered, kicked a field goal and won the game. If this hadn't happened, of course, the coach's skeleton probably would still be rattling from the tallest pine.

But when you study that situation, it makes a bit of sense. Whenever you have only a minute or so to play, it's a long shot, whatever you do. You're deep in your own territory and you must get the ball down to the other end of the field. I suppose a quick-kick is about as good as any other move. I'd just as soon the enemy have the ball on his own five-yard line with two minutes to play, as to have it myself on our own 20. Even if he has possession, we're looking at only five yards separating us from victory.

Zones of Field Position

For *Field Position* teaching, most coaches divide the field into three zones. The 35-yard lines are the division points. From our own goal out to our 35 is the Critical Zone. Different coaches have different names for it. Probably it should be called the Ulcer Zone because that's what it breeds among coaches pacing the sidelines and worrying if their team is going to get the dickens out of there!

The last 35 yards we call the Scoring Zone. This is where you pick up an added advantage. You gain an extra down. The down you saved for punting in the Critical Zone and the Middle Zone now becomes a full-grown friend. You may use four downs to make your necessary 10 yards now, because you probably won't have to punt.

The middle section is a free-wheeling area where we put on a show for the spectators.

Some coaches have divided the field even further.

They'll have a zone (usually the first 20 yards from their own goal) where they'll kick on third down, if there are at least five yards to go. Then, some set the final five yards of the field into another zone—one where the quarterback usually carries the ball himself, or feeds it on a simple handoff, avoiding the pulling of linemen and other involvements.

But we stay with three simple zones.

Escape Route from the Critical Zone

Now, in the Critical Zone, we're interested in only one thing: Get the ball out of there. Here is where one mistake will break your back.

We are not thinking about scoring when we're in the Critical Zone. Our quarterback is concerned with one idea; get the ball back on the far side of the 50-yard line without giving it up. (This doesn't include punting across the 50. Move it on the other side of the 50 with your offense, *then* your punt takes on added weight.)

Here is where we want conservative plays and not those double reverses and wild pitchouts that invite fumbles. We can't afford mistakes because they may be crammed down our throats and emerge up on the scoreboard.

The quarterback has done a masterful job if he gets the ball into the other fellow's yard before he must punt.

Once you're across the 50, you feel like an unsaddled horse. You can breathe deeply again. Let the other team take the ball after your punt and start his offense. You know the odds are against his scoring on you. Yet back there inside your own 35, the odds were heavily in his favor, if some mistake gave him possession.

The Longest Way Home

Most touchdowns come after a fumble, a pass interception, a blocked punt, or a losing gamble.

If your opponent's scores always follow a kickoff or a punt, then you're in good shape. Your quarterback is doing a splendid job. He hasn't made the mistake of calling plays that encourage fumbles.

Occasionally, a fumble will simply foam up and happen. Your ball carrier will sometimes be knocked loose from the ball, even if he had all four arms wrapped around it and stitched neatly inside his jersey. Usually if you fumble in the Scoring Zone, it won't be held against you. But if you fumble in the Critical Zone, a prayer meeting is in order.

You *must* force the other team to drive 50 yards or more for his score. Then it's not a "cheap" touchdown. Any time he has to move only 35 yards or less, then it's a "cheap" score handed to him on a silver platter of yielded *Field Position.*

Six Years of Texas' Field Position

1. ***The Cheap Touchdown.*** For an example, let's look at the figures on the first six years our staff operated at the University of Texas.

- *In 1957,* the Texas defense yielded three "cheap" touchdowns during the regular season. We lost two games in which we handed over the ball in our Critical Zone. *But* our opponents handed us *seven* cheap scores and we escaped with a 6-3-1 season.
- In the *Sugar Bowl* that year, we gave up three cheapies to Mississippi and got ourselves slaughtered as a result.
- *In 1958,* Texas yielded seven easy scores and received only three in return. We had a 7-3 season.
- *In 1959,* we allowed only *two* cheapies and collected *eight* from the foes and this was rather important in a 9-1 season.
- *In 1960,* we handed over four cheap scores in return for five. The season: 7-3 again.

• *In 1961*, Texas gave up just two gift packages of 35 yards or less. But we cashed in on 12 from the other teams, in a 9-1 season.

• *In 1962*, we allowed only one cheap touchdown and one cheap field goal, and we received five in return. The record: 9-0-1.

You can readily see the influence of cheap touchdowns in the season's record. In three seasons where we won nine games, we gave up only two cheap scores each year, while collecting a total of 25 from opponents.

2. ***Average Length of Scoring Drives.*** Perhaps a better way to judge the success of *Field Position* is to note how far the scoring drives averaged. How far did you force the other guy to grunt and grind for his scores? And how far did you have to move for yours?

Take a look:

- 1957—Opp. TD drive average: 54 yds.
  Texas average: 43 yds.
- 1958—Opp. TD drive average: 55 yds.
  Texas average: 53 yds.
- 1959—Opp. TD drive average: 56 yds.
  Texas average: 49 yds.
- 1960—Opp. TD drive average: 50 yds.
  Texas average: 51 yds.
- 1961—Opp. TD drive average: 66 yds.
  Texas average: 53 yds.
- 1962—Opp. TD drive average: 59 yds.
  Texas average: 55 yds.

You can readily see why 1959, 1961 and 1962 were the most successful years. Our opponents had to work harder for their touchdowns.

In 1961, our touchdown drive average was a bit higher than usual because we had a more explosive offense and several long touchdown runs by Saxton and Cook.

And in 1962, our opponents played *Field Position*

Figure 15: Score one for the defense! A fumble recovered by Perry McWilliams in the end zone in the 1962 Texas-Oklahoma game gave us one of five "cheap" touchdowns for that season and the first six points in a 9-6 win. The Texas defense scored all the points in this match.

pretty successfully against us. Nothing came easy that year, as sometimes it had with the quick-footed boys.

With Weak Offense, Field Position Is Vital

But whenever your runners are not very talented or fast, you'll play the kicking game more and you'll pay more attention to *Field Position*. You'll work harder to get the ball back on the far side of the 50 so the other guy can make the mistakes.

Of course, as I've said before, this sometimes isn't the most popular football to the spectators.

People are sometimes hard put to understand that kicking is a method of moving the ball up and down the field, just like running it or throwing it. And that most of your games are won by the other fellow's mistakes, and your ability to capitalize on them.

Pleasing the Fans Is Risky Business

Regardless of trends and success stories, coaches cannot hope to please all the experts in the $5 seats.

And I believe most college coaches are like this old Scotsman who had come down from the braes to shop for an anvil:

> He was a wee close wi' his guineas as becomes a hodden-gray highlander. It ain't every blessed day a mon must part wi' his life savings for an anvil.
>
> After much bickerin' prattle, he found a bargain, clasped the heavy iron to his bosom and started home.
>
> His route led across a footlog above a raging stream. He lost his balance and tumbled in.
>
> Sandy came to the top, gasped for breath and yelled, "Help!" as any honest mon would, and vanished under the water.

Again he surfaced and cried, "Somebody help me!" and submerged again.

The third time, Sandy fought his way, spewed out a gallon of water and yelled, with considerable anger, "If someone dunna help me, I'll be dropping this anvil!"

And this is about the way college coaches, or most of them, feel about *Field Position* and all its everlasting logic. For all the criticism it may draw, they're not going to drop that logical anvil until someone finds a better way to influence the standings.

Maybe it's not the romantic way. But we'll leave that to John Wayne and Cary Grant. The won-lost column is the most realistic reading that I know.

chapter ten

The Quarterback: A Young Friend in Need

None of us in the coaching fraternity spends as much time with his quarterbacks as he should, or, as he'd prefer.

But it is not the coach's fault. He'd like to adopt the young men; keep them on a leash; and bombard them constantly with footballisms. However, a college quarterback is not just a college quarterback, period. He is a young man of many facets.

Requirements of Normal Social Life

He is a student and probably a very good student interested in his course of study and in his future after college. Because he is of quarterback capabilities, chances are he is also a campus leader with a full load of social and extra-

curricular activities. You may be quite sure he has a girl friend or several, a habit not especially limited to quarterbacks.

A quarterback's life is not the full-time football life the coach leads. A coach may think, eat, and sleep football. A quarterback must mix in other components if he is to receive a well-rounded college education. Therefore, a coach usually is limited to a couple personal sessions with his quarterbacks each week. It's not enough, of course, but it has to suffice.

Sessions with the Quarterback

Most of that time, I try to spend on the listening end. I can lecture to quarterbacks for hours, but I can't tell if

they are absorbing all this exalted wisdom I'm spouting. The only way I can determine their grasp of concepts is to call them into my office, prop my feet up and prompt *them* to pop off.

I want them to tell *me* about our next opponent. I want to know about his defensive tendencies, what he usually does under certain conditions and at certain times. I want to know what our plans are to overcome his strength and exploit his weaknesses.

Of course, all this information has been told to the squad earlier in the week. I want to know if the quarterbacks have adopted this knowledge and have solutions to the problems at hand. It's the only way I know to measure what a quarterback has absorbed.

Now these sessions (the big one comes on Friday) are usually for junior and senior quarterbacks. Some of the sophomore answers might frighten me into another line of business.

I don't believe there is such an animal as a "natural" quarterback or a "born" quarterback. Certainly the quarterback types have certain natural gifts, such as intelligence, leadership, poise, and confidence. These are the first qualities you look for in a quarterback, before physical talent.

But there are those certain logics of *whys* that he must be taught.

For that reason, in our office sessions, we don't limit our questions to offensive plans for certain situations in the upcoming game. We want him to analyze our opponent's defensive game and tell us *why* he has these plans.

All these questions, he should know from previous chats when the coach is doing the talking. But it's not enough that he spout automatic answers like a parrot. We ask him to explain the logic behind the answers. We want him thinking.

Foundation of Logic

Many coaches establish set rules for their quarterbacks. Some meticulously draw off the field into several zones. The first 10 yards away from your own goal line, for example, is the five-yard-average zone. You must average five yards each on your first two plays if you are to hold the ball. If you don't, then the quarterback is to punt on third down.

From the 10-yard line to the 20, you must average 3.4 yards.

In the middle of the field, the required average drops to 3.2 yards per carry, etc. Coaches also list exact play selection plans to be followed in each of these zones.

We don't require those rigid standards of our quarterbacks, but we do expect them to have a solid foundation of football logic.

We want the quarterback to understand fully the kicking game. We don't tell him to kick one down earlier for every touchdown lead he has, as some coaches teach. But we do want him to realize that the quick-kick is a bold, aggressive move. And we want him to understand *why* it is.

We like to hear him explain why the chances of a successful pass decrease with each successive down of a series. *Why* his bootleg pass should be worked off his most successful ground play. *Why* he should keep repeating the same play against a stunting defense. *Why*, on clutch plays, he should give the ball to his best ball carrier behind his best blocker. *Why* poor field position calls for conservative plays.

We want the quarterback to understand there must be a reason behind *every* play called.

Then, we want to hear his thinking on possible emergencies. How a change in weather will alter his game plans, or an injury to his ace fullback, perhaps.

Quarterback Comprehension: Measure of Coach's Success

A great measure of a coach's success is determined by how well he makes himself understood to his players, especially his quarterbacks.

I believe this is the strongest quality of Bud Wilkinson at Oklahoma. He has a way of expressing himself that leaves no question in a player's mind. By the time a quarterback graduates from Oklahoma, he automatically thinks the way Coach Wilkinson does.

And this is one of the real thrills in coaching. You're standing on the sideline in a clutch situation, without the chance to rush information in to your quarterback. And you're praying, "Gosh, I hope he calls the fullback trap. They're set up for it. I wish I could signal to him."

And sure enough, the huddle breaks and your team lines up and runs the fullback trap. It's a good feeling.

The Old Theme: Simplicity

Here again, we try to keep our play designations as simple as possible. We're still striving to eliminate confusion. If our quarterback is calling the right end sweep off the Flip-Flop offense, he merely says, "Right 18," and then gives the snap signal. "Right" tells us the strong side, and "18" is the sweep, regardless of right or left.

We don't do a lot of automatic signal calling, where the original play is changed by the quarterback at the line of scrimmage, usually to a trap play or a quick pass. Of course, we have automatic plays and we've had some success with them. But this is an operation that requires a lot of time, so that your quarterback may attain the poise and confidence of using the switch-off signals, and the entire team has the ability to pick up quickly the change in assignments without confusion. But I've seen occasions when automatic signals would cause confusion one time out of three. And if there's confusion, it's just not worth it.

I'd rather our quarterback just guess at a play, guess at the defensive alignment, and then come out of the huddle and run that play regardless of how the defense has shifted. It may be that you're running squarely into your opponent's strength, but at least your players know their assignments. To me, this is better than running away from the strength and having some of your players confused on their new blocking assignments. Again, it gets back to the old law that a confused player cannot be aggressive.

Eliminate the Negative

Basically your successful quarterback is one who knows his personnel, their abilities and faults, who forever keeps in mind the down and the distance required for a first down, the score, the weather, the wind and the clock . . . one who knows when to adjust the tempo of the game, who knows when to take chances and when to play conservatively, and one who fully understands the kicking game.

Good signal-calling, to me, doesn't mean that the quarterback comes up with a brilliant call. Those are rare birds. The coach or the quarterback seldom make those brilliant play selections. The play may have great success, but not because the quarterback had a brain storm. It had great success because it was executed well, or because the opponent made a mistake.

So the mark of a good quarterback is not the brilliance of his selections. *It is his ability to stay away from the stupid calls.*

There are many more opportunities for blunders than for brilliance. Your lad must shun those don't-have-a-chance plays. He must forget the temptation to be a genius, for more often than not, he'll wind up with mud on his face.

Gambling Prohibited

The gambling quarterback, like the dodo bird, is fast disappearing from the American scene. College quarterbacks have a disciplined set of guidance rules, and there is no such thing as a gamble in professional football.

Quarterbacks now run an orderly huddle, undisturbed by some of the freelance opinions that used to spice up the old days. Like that miserable afternoon in 1916, when

Georgia Tech was murdering Cumberland, 222-0, in the highest football score of all time.

> Late in the fourth quarter, Cumberland managed to receive a kickoff without fumbling and the quarterback suggested a halfback sweep.
>
> "Gosh, no," gasped the halfback. "The last time we tried that, the linebacker broke two of my ribs."
>
> Okay, said the quarterback, the other halfback off-tackle. "Anything but that," moaned the other halfback. "That guard already has busted my nose and loosened two teeth."
>
> Well, the fullback up the middle.
>
> "Nope, not me," said the fullback. "I'm solid bruises now. I couldn't run a step."
>
> There was a short awkward silence, while the quarterback tried to think of a compromise.
>
> "Say," a weary guard suggested timidly, "couldn't we just throw a long, incomplete pass?"

Coaching the Defensive Quarterback

Defensive coaches should spend just as much time with the defensive signal-caller as the offense teachers spend with quarterbacks. But they seldom do.

They should go through the same routines exactly, the sessions in which the defensive leader explains what he will do in certain situations and why. Actually, the defensive signal-caller is ordering a play, anticipating what the offense is going to do. The offense is calling a play anticipating what the defense is going to do. They're matching wits.

If you haven't spent as much time with that defensive signal-caller, then he's at a disadvantage with the opposing quarterback.

You look for the same leadership traits in the defensive leader. And certainly he must understand offense.

When the Dallas Cowboys hired Tom Landry to coach their new entry in the National Football League, they held the usual press conference. And one of the questions asked Tom was, "You were a defensive coach with the New York *Giants.* Do you consider yourself qualified to coach offense as well?"

"You must first know offense," said Tom gently, "before you can coach defense."

The defensive signal-caller, usually one of the linebackers, should have a solid knowledge of all the problems running through the offensive quarterback's mind.

He should be just as thoroughly briefed as your quarterback. He must understand his opponents' capabilities from different formations, and the capabilities of the personnel involved.

His preparation from the scouting report should be just as painstakingly complete as that of the offensive quarterback.

Generally, the leader of defense must decide whether to use the containing or penetrating techniques, or a combination of both, on a particular play. But he, too, must always have in mind that old check-list: down and distance, weather, scoreboard, clock, and all the knowledge the quarterback needs.

Down in his own territory, he must think ahead of the offense. What was their favorite play in this drive? Who is their best ball carrier? Who is their best blocker? In the big clutch, isn't this the play that will be called?

Here, too, the *stupid call* must be avoided.

In fact, a blundering gamble on a defensive play can be even more costly than on offense. The offense may lose a down and yardage. But the defense may lose a score.

Coaches Calling Signals—A Helping Hand?

Several seasons ago, an Oklahoma City writer named Volney Meece asked me, "How much sideline play calling do you do?"

"I do about as much," I answered, "as the coaches who claim they don't do any."

All coaches do a certain amount of sideline play selections.

Some coaches argue that's taking the game away from the boys, making robots out of them.

"Kids should make their own decisions. That's part of the lesson learned in football." I have heard this statement many times from fellow coaches.

I question sometimes whether these coaches adhere 100 percent to this high-sounding ethic.

I've heard some of these coaches deplore the use of "wild card" substitutions to call plays. Or bitterly denounce a signal from the bench for a particular offensive selection. Yet these same coaches (and I know specific examples) will turn right around and call every *defensive* alignment used by their team.

So what's the difference? Is it okay to call the defensive alignments, but a purple sin to call the offense?

Is there a coach who hasn't swung his foot to signal a punt to his quarterback, or yelled at his secondary to back up on a passing down? I'd like to see one of those citizens, if one exists.

All coaches call some plays from the sidelines. Some are more open about it. And sometimes they're mistaken in their selections, also.

Claude Gilstrap, the witty coach at Arlington State College, likes to tell about the time his quarterback was searching frantically for a sideline signal to meet a ticklish situation.

"It was during a time out and this kid kept looking at me from the field, and I'd look in the other direction. He'd come a little closer to the sideline and yell at me, but I'd slide down the bench and look off. Finally, he came over to the bench and asked what he should call on the next play.

"I told him, 'Listen, son, you got a four-year scholarship and I got a one-year contract. Make your own decisions.' "

A Will and a Way

The Rules Committee outlawed the "wild card" substitutions before the 1963 season, whereby a coach could send in one or two players after any down. There were explanations that this would stop sideline play-calling. Of course, this argument doesn't exactly hold water. If a coach wants to call plays from the sidelines, he is going to call plays from the sidelines and there's not much you can do to stop him. There are all sorts of possible methods.

We played once against a coach who selected almost every play. He kept his reserve quarterback sitting by him on a sideline chair, in front of the bench. The idle quarterback would relay the play selection to the quarterback in action by a simple system of signals, not unlike the signs a baseball coach flashes from the coaches' box. He might touch his left elbow and then his helmet, or pound his right knee with his left fist, and any other simple maneuver.

Nope, legislation won't do it. Where there's a will to call signals, there will always be a way.

Coaching from the Pressbox

We like to have both an offensive coach and a defensive coach on the pressbox phone during the game, if they are available.

It's difficult to see the offensive and defensive alignments from the sideline perspective. Of course the sideline coach always has knowledge that he doesn't have to see, such as the wind, Field Position, the score, the knowledge of his own personnel, etc.

But the coaches in the pressbox help greatly when our opponents change an offensive formation, for example. Our defense might not be making the proper adjustment to a man-in-motion or we may be playing our end too wide or too tight.

Also, from the sideline, we can give help to the pressbox coaches over the phone. We can tip them on what the next play will be and they can watch for certain reactions from the opponents. It works both ways.

The Hectic Sideline, When Confusion Helps

I'm afraid, however, that we don't keep a very tidy sideline on the Texas side of the field. We have a lot of confusion in our bench area. It's not like the Mississippi bench, where the players sit all the time in well-disciplined rows. Nor the Rice bench, which is run along the same orderly lines.

As a coaching staff, we've worried about this bench discipline quite a bit. Our players on the sideline were always standing up, running up and down in front of the bench, whooping and stomping. And this created confusion.

In 1961 we turned over a new leaf. We were determined to run an orderly bench. Okay, everybody sit down and stay down. Nobody stands up unless you're called by one of the coaches.

Then, in an early game when the going got hot, they piled off the bench and started their pep rally. I had to beat 'em back and it was difficult to do without a baseball bat. But they finally returned to the bench and sat down. They stayed there meekly enough until the next hot spot came along, and here they came again.

We gave up. It's tough to try to knock down that enthusiasm. I suppose I'd just as soon be a little confused and unorganized and have that pep among the players.

Sometimes I may have trouble finding a substitute or making myself heard over the noise. But if I call a player's name, the other boys will find him for me. I don't have to search for him. We also make the boys keep up with their own substitute status, when they can re-enter a game and when they can't. It's impossible for us to keep track of it.

We live in a sideline confusion. But this is one exception, we think, where confusion helps aggression rather than hinders it.

chapter eleven

Practices: Year-Round, Well-Planned

As I have mentioned before, one of the toughest parts of a head coach's job is presiding over the practice schedule. It is his decision how long to work a team; how the temperature is affecting them; and whether to use contact work as late as Wednesday. Many of these decisions must be made on the spot, and they may vary from week to week.

Drills That Are Not All Drudgery

Football teams are built, they say, in spring drills and polished in the fall. Saturdays are the fun days. Of course, the spring workouts and the two-a-day drills that precede regular fall sessions are the drudgery.

As a player, I can never remember when football practice wasn't fun. Even spring practice. Some people argue that workouts are more of a grind today, because of the more organized approach and the detailed scheduling of drills.

There has been a theory on the decline of baseball interest throughout the country—that there is too much of it; that youngsters start playing kid baseball by the time they are able to lift a glove. And by the time they've played a dozen years, they are soured on the game and don't even want to serve as spectators.

Football doesn't face that danger, if it is such. Perhaps if football practice lasted the year round, boys might weary of it. But now, even spring drills are limited. Colleges don't spend nearly the time on the practice field that they once did.

Add a Little Fun

Most coaches make a conscious effort to make the workouts fun. Bobby Dodd advises a coach to find a natural comedian on the squad and encourage him to keep the squad "loosey-goosey." Duffy Daugherty has a special award at Michigan State, called the Oil Can, and he presents it each year to the squad member with the best sense of humor, the one who has contributed most to the squad morale.

Duffy also started something else. He has a 15-minute break during practice in which the players may do whatever they want. The guards can practice punting, or the ends may throw passes, or everybody can flop down in the shade and puff. Of course, Duff has a different approach altogether from most coaches. He may tell jokes in the dressing room right before a game. He seldom seems serious.

At Texas, we don't encourage comedians. I don't want comic relief to get out of control. I don't discourage jokes or keep boys throttled down if there's something they want to say. But I don't want the situation to get to an informal point where they're running up and giving me a hotfoot. Like every other squad, we have some silly little traditions, like nicknames or a little applause routine. If somebody busts a signal or goofs, a player will yell, "How about three for old Fred?" and the squad will clap three times. Just something to keep it from being too grim.

But the only way I know how to keep football fun is to win. That's the only answer. There is no laughter in losing.

Don't Overwork the Team

Certainly there is a danger in overwork. Before Texas' 1962 *Cotton Bowl* game with Mississippi, we just horsed around. Our workouts weren't too organized, just enough running to stay in shape. I didn't want a go-go-go atmosphere. We had just finished a tough 10-game schedule, so we limited the hard work to four or five days. And there was a reason, a big one.

Our first year at Texas, we were invited to play Old Miss in the *Sugar Bowl*. The *Rebels* were mighty and bold and everyone presumed the *Longhorns* were headed for the slaughterhouse.

I worked the squad too hard. I tried to get in another spring practice. The team got ready to play four or five days too soon, and sure enough we went to the slaughterhouse. I learned something from that. You always learn something when you get boxed around, namely, that when we have to prepare for a bowl game, we will mainly keep the boys running a lot and limit contact work to just a few days.

The Challenge Tests

Some coaches, such as Bryant at Alabama and Owens at Washington, make use of "challenge" sessions at workouts, to spice up the drills and to stimulate competition on the squad.

If a second team guard thinks he is a better man than the player ahead of him, he may challenge him to a contest. Usually it is a block-and-tackle contest. The challenger will try to block his opponent on three plays, one-on-one style. And then the first stringer will try to block the challenger on three plays. If the challenger beats his man in a majority of the six jousts, then he may replace him on the first team.

Also, Bryant has used an idea called the "challenge board." We worked with it some at Mississippi State. It is simply a flat board laid on the ground. The challenger stands with his feet straddling the board at one end, and his teammate at the other. They approach each other, with their feet kept on either side of the board and see which one can knock the other over, or back, or to one side.

This is mostly a mental conditioner and we don't use it anymore. For one thing, this sort of drill requires only one effort. We're looking for the boy who gives the third and fourth effort on each play.

These challenge drills don't tell you what a boy will do on punt coverage when nobody is watching him. Anybody will fight if people are looking at him. But we search for the boy who will scrap in the middle of the line, unseen by the coach, teammate, spectator, or anybody else.

Too, strength isn't everything. At Mississippi State, we had a big tackle who was always challenging the players ahead of him at his position. And he would get on that challenge board and manhandle them. Then, he'd want to know why he wasn't playing first string. He was too awkward.

Also, there are many different tests of courage. You'll find boys who wouldn't fight anybody with their fists, yet were vicious football players. And you can find Golden Gloves heavyweights who shy away from football contact. Also, there are good tough football players who don't have enough courage to push themselves away from the dinner table at the right time.

If you're going to use challenge tests to determine if a second teamer can move ahead, it probably should be conducted on some sort of obstacle course, to include all sorts of toughness. You'd probably cut down on the number of challengers, also.

Liven Up the Spring Drills

Spring practice is pretty much drudgery, no matter how much camouflage you stack around it. Some coaches have advanced the idea of playing a split football season, in the fall and in the spring. I don't think much of that idea, but there does seem to be some merit in one game, just to keep up the players' interest. Many schools have a varsity-alumni game to serve that purpose.

Spring practice, of course, is where you build your football team; where you install any changes; and where you judge your incoming personnel. And it's admittedly a grind. We are limited to 20 days of spring drills in our conference, and we try to have three intra-squad game scrimmages to liven up the drills.

But we try to preach this to the squad: Spring practice is competitive, just as the Saturday games in the Fall. I tell the players that this very afternoon, over in College Station, the *Aggies* are going through a Spring drill and they're just as tired and sore as we are. Up at Waco, Baylor is doing the same thing. Everybody is wishing this Spring practice would hurry and finish.

Well, our success next Fall depends largely on whether Texas players are willing to work harder this very afternoon than the *Aggies* are working at College Station or the *Horned Frogs* are working at Fort Worth. We try to convince players that they're not just putting in a day's work and jumping under a shower before they run off to make springtime calf-eyes at a coed. They are actually *competing* with the other schools on this hot, lazy Spring afternoon. If a team wants to excel, hard Spring work is something it must do.

Provide Competition in the Summer

After Spring drills, we try to carry that theme of competition through the summer months. Woody Hayes once said that man reaches greatness only when he has to compete to his full potential, either in sports, the classroom, business, or hop-scotch. If you can persuade a boy to work out on his own time during the hot summer months, you are making him attack greatness with brass knuckles.

Keep Your Drill Program Flexible

In 1962, the Rice *Owls* had played four games without a victory, although they had tied LSU in the opener. In their fourth game, they were beaten by an underdog Southern Methodist team that hadn't won either. Coach

Jess Neely threw away his customary Monday practice procedure. Usually Mondays are devoted to light workouts for the players who competed the previous Saturday, and any contact work is limited to reserves.

But on the Monday preceding the Texas game, Coach Neely sent his regulars through the roughest scrimmage of the year. He wasn't satisfied with their performance against SMU, so he toughened the workout routine. Witnesses said the *Owls* hit harder than they had all season. And it must have done the job.

Rice was nine feet tall when we played them the following Saturday night. We hadn't lost a game and the *Owls* hadn't won. But the score was 14-14.

A Variety of Theories

So—there may be all sorts of theories about workout planning. Coach Hayes at Ohio State believes you can keep boys on the field no longer than two hours and get maximum results. He holds that college boys just don't have that many shots in their physical locker. And if you want maximum effort out of each boy on each play, in practice as well as in the game, then work them two hours and let them go.

Jock Sutherland said that the coach who constantly griped at his players in practice was unsure of himself and his team.

There are so many thoughts and theories about how to handle the mental and physical conditioning of a team, that we don't subscribe to any rigid set of rules. Possibly you would call it "coaching by the seat of your pants," but we try to be flexible.

True, this leads to indecision. Sometimes it's hard to tell whether you've worked a team too hard, or whether you haven't worked it enough. An over-trained, stale team has the same physical appearance as a team that's not in shape. The legs lack spring.

Of course, I believe there must be some contact work

in each week's preparation. Some coaches like an open date preceding their Big Game of the season. I don't know if this is good or bad. You still must have contact work and the danger of injury is just as prevalent in practice as it is in a game. Probably more so. A player may be more apt to relax and get careless in practice.

Football Drills Have to be Tough

So, we believe that practices have to be tough. If football didn't demand sternness and toughness, everybody would be a champion. You'll find players vowing that Saturday games are frolics compared to practice sessions. I'm always reminded of the grizzled old Army sergeant who was leading a squad to the top of an island ridge. Japanese fire forced the Yanks to crawl on their bellies and squirm behind every rock and bush. The heat, the bugs, the dust, and the enemy bullets were making life miserable and a rookie private was complaining.

"Huh, if you think this is tough," said the sergeant, "you should have been on maneuvers in Louisiana."

chapter twelve

The Hectic Weekly Schedule

A work week consists of five or six days with the seventh day for rest. This, of course, doesn't apply to coaches working on football game films and scouting reports.

No Rest for the Coach

An autumn Sunday is one of the busiest days in a football coach's week. Certainly he'd like to spend it as a day of rest, reading the funnies, romping with the kids, watching television, as do the more civilized tribes in America. Instead, he must get a good running start on next week's work.

About the only hours a coach has for relaxation during the season come immediately after the game on Saturday. And if you play night games, as we often do in Texas, then even those few free hours are severely rationed.

Several seasons ago, my particular Sundays were tailor-made for the madhouse. They began at 8 a.m., included Sunday School with Edith and the kids (Marian, Mack and David), a brief meeting with the staff, a chartered plane flight to Houston, 100 miles away, for a live television show, the flight back, and staff meetings and film reviews until late Sunday night.

This schedule has been alleviated somewhat. In 1961, I began taping my weekly television show in Austin and films of the show were then shipped to the five or six stations over the state which used it. This eliminated the Houston trip. Then, I was able to spend a leisurely Sunday morning with my family (after the television chore) and even have a civilized lunch before reporting to the athletic

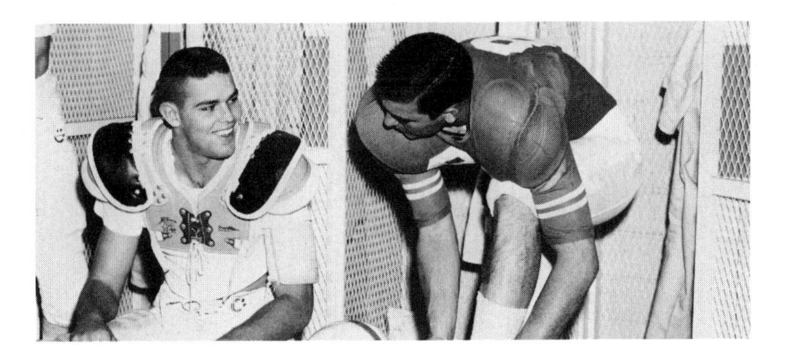

offices for the next whirl of the football merry-go-round.

We don't see our players after Saturday's game until the following Monday afternoon. Often we leave them on their own after out-of-town games, if they wish. For example, the Oklahoma-Texas game is played annually in Dallas as a feature of the State Fair. After the game, the players can fly back to Austin on the chartered plane if they wish, or they may go to their homes to visit parents or friends. All we ask is that they get back on the campus Sunday night in time to get a good night's sleep and be ready for classes Monday morning.

Reviewing Films

But the coaches—they're horses of a different color; or oxen in another ditch. We'll meet around 2 o'clock Sunday afternoon for our everlasting devotion to eyestrain. Our game films are available 2½ hours after we deliver them to the developing laboratory in Austin. It's possible, after an afternoon game at home, to have the game films for study Saturday night. But we skip that. It would simply mean more work for the divorce courts.

Sunday afternoon, we start off by studying the previous day's film as a staff. Then the individual coaches will study their specialties—linebackers, offensive backs, etc.

By Sunday night, the game films of our next opponent have arrived and they go on the projector. In the Southwest Conference, we have an agreement to exchange game films. An extra copy of our game film is printed right after the game, and shipped by air to our next opponent. The opponent does likewise. Sometimes, according to individual agreements, we exchange films of the *two* previous games.

The staff will eyeball the next week's foe for a couple hours and get sufficiently frightened by 11 P.M. so that we're able to toss and turn properly that night.

The Private Eyes

Monday is a whingdinger. I write a letter to the Ex-

Students Association and the Longhorn Club (a booster organization) in the morning, while the other coaches are breaking down the game film into the three divisions—offense, defense, kicking—and drawing up the tackle charts and studying the scouting reports on the next enemy.

We *must* get our future general plans completed Monday, so we can start work on them Tuesday: whatever personnel changes we will make, the new plays we'll install, and the special defenses we'll rig up—all must be done Monday.

Monday evening is our only night squad meeting of the week. This is when our squad sees the film of the last game. As I said, they don't see the game in sequence and they don't see it in one group.

The offensive backfield coaches take the backs in one room and show the movie, while the line coaches take the linemen into another room to show another copy of the film. This allows us to get all of our offensive corrections out of the way at one time, saving precious minutes. (We have six copies made of each game film.)

Defensively, the secondary, the down linemen, and the ends—linebackers are separated and shown the films in three rooms at the same time. The secondary, of course, sees film shot with a wide-angle lens so that they can better see the over-all coverage picture.

By breaking down the squad into these groups for individual showing, we get concentrated coverage. Each boy sees himself on offense, with one set of coaches giving corrections. Then he joins another set of coaches for the defensive comments.

If we simply showed the game to the squad in natural sequence, it would be a harem-scarem operation, with defensive coaches talking now, and then offensive coaches, and then kicking comments. There would be no singleness of purpose.

All plays involving kicking and kick coverage, as I mentioned, are separated and joined on a separate reel to be shown later on in the week. (After things have settled down to a steady roar.)

Detours Ahead

Our general, over-all program is planned on Monday, but our particular drill philosophy is based on a day-to-day plan. We don't sit down on Monday and plan the entire week's practice. We sit down on Monday morning and plan Monday afternoon's drills, and after that, we fly by the seat of our well-worn pants.

After each practice, the staff meets and takes stock of what was accomplished that day, how much progress was made on this defense or that certain run-pass option play. If one of the coaches isn't satisfied with the progress on his particular project, then we'll schedule more time on it the next day.

That's the reason I'm unable to give a real thoughtful answer when someone asks about the trends of football, the motivation of certain ideas in seasons to come. I'm too busy worrying about the next day's practice. I can't even tell the progress of our own team, much less football as a whole. I've never been a believer in long-range plans, anyway. Tomorrow is here today.

When in Doubt . . .

As the week progresses, doubts begin to pile up in the mind of every coach.

Oscar Levant once said about a certain President: "Once he's made up his mind, he's full of indecision."

The closer to game time, the more you begin to second-guess yourself. I sincerely envy the coach who can be confident on the eve of a game. I'm always scared. I never get the feeling that everything is all set, that our team is honestly ready to play the game. We always have the worry that there was *something* we should have done to complete our preparation.

Maybe the squad hasn't thought about this game enough. Maybe it's not taking the game seriously enough.

Do you think we've run enough wind sprints this week? Or maybe we've run too many? Do the boys look a bit tired? Maybe we worked them too hard on Wednesday? Will Johnny Doakes' ankle go out on him the first time he makes the cut on the sweep? Will the quarterbacks remember that the trap play will never go if that slow-charging No. 64 is in the game? Maybe we should have worked more on the screen pass? By game time the staff is a bit shaky. Just before kickoff, I really don't know what I want. Playing the game was never like this.

The Night Before the Game

A winning team has to be a close-knit crew. We try to draw the players closer and closer together with each day of game preparation, in the same way you would wind a top. The closer to kickoff, the tighter we want that feeling of team togetherness.

The night before a home game, we take the squad away from the campus, to a motel on the outskirts of Austin. We have better control over the boys there. If we want to hold meetings, we don't have to chase anybody down. They are all there under one roof. We can control the telephone calls and the disrupting visits from the constant well-wishers who are not always too considerate just before game time.

It is strictly *football, football, football* until the game is over. If some players have a Saturday morning class, a student manager drives them to the college and then brings them back to the squad.

Separate the Players from Outsiders

Then we draw the knot even closer. There are other people around us at the motel, but once we get into the dressing room, the outsiders are trimmed off. It is just the squad, and just before the kickoff, the circle boils down to the guys who are going to do the playing. We want those adrenal glands excited and spurting all sorts of magic substances into the bloodstream and producing an "adrenal kick" that brings out unexpected strength. The tighter our circle is packed, the bigger the explosion.

Responsible Players After the Game

After the game, the squad is dismissed until Monday. We try to give players the responsibility of their own discipline, as a coach can't guard his squad all the time.

"If I ever have to lock my boys in at night," says Bobby Dodd, "I'll quit."

A coach likes to feel that players more or less keep each other in line. I had some trouble in this direction the first season at Texas, but there's been none since, thank goodness. I've said before that the ideal football squad has 15 or 20 seniors. The more mature players are important monitors. That's another reason it's so important to keep players in school for all four years. We make a special effort not only to keep the boys in school for four years of football, but to encourage them to get that degree. I give a personal gift, a ring with a white "T" on an orange setting, to each football player who gets his sheepskin. Unashamedly, I stole the idea from Bear Bryant.

Coaches try to instill the feeling of individual responsibility. If one player gets out of line, stays out late or goes on wild parties, the entire squad should resent it. Usually, a few of the older players will have a visit with the boy. Unless a player wants to make the sacrifices necessary to excel and be accepted by his teammates, you're not going to keep him from breaking training. He'll do it. But that boy isn't of much value to a winning team, anyway.

chapter thirteen

In the corner of the hotel mezzanine was a large blackboard and a short compact man with the face of a dance hall bouncer was scribbling some weird hieroglyphics.

The board had been used for the X's and O's of football diagramming among players and coaches gathered in New York for the Look magazine All-America presentations.

But this young fireplug was writing in another code—a bunch of ssssses and yyyys and parentheses and plusses and minuses. Photographers were firing away madly. The photographers had demanded, "Write down some science stuff, Joe."

So Joe Romig, the dedicated All-America guard from Colorado in 1960-61, was writing down some science stuff. At least that's what he said it was. To some of us, it looked amazingly like a Betty Crocker recipe for corn fritters.

The Scholastic Look

A New Breed of Players

The photographers wanted a change from the usual poses of All-Americans in New York, signing autographs, posing with a pretty girl, or gazing up at the tall buildings.

Therefore Romig was obliging by chalking up the formula for figuring the area of an irregular surface, bounded by a straight line and an arc. And there was an audience of several husky young men looking on critically.

"There," said Romig, a serious student of nuclear physics at Colorado. The blackboard was covered with turkey tracks and the problem was finished.

A tall youth studied the blackboard with chin cupped in one large hand. "I think you missed it, Joe," said be-

spectacled Greg Mather, the *Navy* end. He picked up the chalk and made several alterations. Now it looked like the Betty Crocker recipe for pumpkin pie.

A short time afterward, Alex Kroll, a hulk from Rutgers and an honor student in English literature, walked over to Romig. "Mather is wrong," he said. "Your first answer was right." Merlin Olsen, the giant tackle from Utah State, agreed with Kroll.

A Lasting Impression

I'll never forget that scene. Times, verily, have changed. Here were these big hunks of muscle, raking over conversations in geophysics and Chaucer, when you might think they'd be talking about off-tackle slants, and girls, and military status, and girls, and pro contracts, and girls.

It reminded me somewhat of a politician's description of the Democratic platform. He said it was like an old hillbilly woman giving a testimonial at a camp meeting.

"I ain't what I oughta be, and I ain't what I'm gonna be," she yelled, "but leastways, I ain't what I was."

Academic Requirements for College Athletes

This is about the story on scholastic requirements for college students. This includes students who weigh 200 pounds and run very fast and who are not adverse to visiting our stadium each autumn Saturday. Some coaches believe the requirements are much too strict; some educators predict they will become even more stringent in the future. But everyone agrees they ain't what they was.

Already there has been a much heavier premium on grades in the past five years and there'll be much more stress on the brainwork in the future. In the past five years at Texas, for example, the entrance requirements for the "second-quarter" student has gone up more than 125 points on his entrance exams. In other words, the student who finishes in the second fourth of his high school graduating class now must score more than 125 points higher on his entrance tests to be admitted to Texas. This is just one example of the tightening-up process.

When I went to college, all the registrar wanted to see was a high school diploma.

Nowadays, when we are recruiting players, we must pay just as much attention to the lad's high school grades as we do to his clocking in the 100-yard dash and how much influence he exerts on the scales.

Birth of the "Brain Coach"

For that reason, we have a comparatively new operation at Texas called "The Brain Coach" and believe me, it's as handy as a pocket on a shirt.

We have a member of our coaching staff who never puts on a T shirt or a baseball cap and who has been no closer to the game of football than the helmet advertisements in a Sears Roebuck catalogue. And yet he's one of the most important members of the staff.

The Background:

1. *Recruiting and Athletics.* When our staff first came to the University of Texas, the team had won only one game the previous autumn.

Some of the alumni were perspiring freely about the gills and were generous with advice on a re-building program.

Many suggested we hire a full-time recruiter as a member of the coaching staff. This is done in many colleges, especially in the Southeast. This staff member simply spends all his time on the road, visiting, scouting, keeping records on hundreds of high school prospects, cementing relations with parents and coaches and alumni. I can think of one university that hires two or three full-time recruiters.

This suggestion came not only from well-meaning alumni, but from some members of the athletic department itself. However, the recruiting rules in the Southwest

Conference are such that this action seemed impractical. We are forbidden even to contact a high school player until he's finished his last game his senior season. In other conferences, like the SEC for example, there is no such prohibition. Prospects can be contacted and visited and courted from junior high school on.

We didn't want to rush into anything like a full-time recruiter. We wanted time to give it some thought.

2. *Academics and Athletics.* Now this was in 1957. I asked for and obtained a list of the Texas freshmen who were recruited in 1953. These would be the seniors of 1956, the year before we arrived at Austin.

We traced the college careers of these boys. How many of them stayed in school to become seniors? Or rather, how many of them remained to become good senior football players? What was the success of those 1953 freshmen?

Then, we moved the research to the following year. We got a list of the 1954 freshmen. These would be the seniors we inherited on the squad. (We had exactly four seniors.)

In studying these figures, these freshmen groups and their individual fates, one fact jumped right out of the research.

It wasn't the *number* of boys that Texas had recruited and brought to the campus. The school had recruited just as many as any other conference school.

We couldn't tell if it was the *caliber* of players recruited. But it was reasonable to presume that the caliber was comparable to other schools.

3. *Recruits, Academics, and Seniors.* But we could tell this: *Not nearly enough of Texas freshmen were becoming seniors and still playing good football.*

They were dropping out along the way. From scholastic requirements, perhaps. From discouragement, perhaps. From lack of interest, perhaps.

But we simply were not getting four seasons of football from the people we recruited.

And I've always believed you must have those 15 or

20 seniors on your squad if you are to have winning seasons. You won't have that many *outstanding* seniors. But out of your freshmen recruits, you should have 15 or 20 still with the squad four years hence. And some of them will naturally be winning football players.

So, our first objective in this Texas program was not to hire a full-time recruiter to flail the bushes and bring in *more* boys.

We needed somebody to help *keep* the boys we recruited. We needed seniors. We needed someone who would help keep the boys in school, keep them passing their courses, *keep them out for football.*

I felt the need was not for a recruiter, but for a counselor. We created that job. The official title is Academic Counselor to Athletes.

The unofficial title is "Brain Coach."

The Position

1. ***What We Did Not Want.*** As far as I know, the Brain Coach at Texas was the first of the breed. There have since been moves in this direction elsewhere, but none which exactly parallel ours.

When we were deciding on the qualifications for our future Academic Counselor to Athletes, we realized that three groups of people would not fill the bill. First, we did not want a man who was ambitious to be a football coach, for he would see the slot as a part-time job helping with the freshman squad which would later lead to a full-time coaching position. If coaching were his goal, then counseling would be only secondary to him, and to us it was definitely primary.

Second, we did not want to hire a graduate student and pay him to take care of the educational counseling, as he would be doing the job solely to make money for his own graduate education. Again, the counseling function would be of secondary significance to him.

Third, hiring a professor on a part-time basis was positively out. We did not want the Brain Coach to be a man who was just out to earn extra money.

2. ***What We Did Want.*** We think the only way we can get an adequate job done is to hire an educator who is not interested in coaching, one who has a sincere interest in devoting full time to guiding young athletes through their college studies.

The late Dr. O. B. Williams, chairman of the athletic council at Texas, knew a fellow named Lan Hewlett who had received his master's degree at the University and was teaching at Lockhart High School. We interviewed Mr. Hewlett, hired him and it might have been the smartest move we ever made.

The Brain Coach has one objective: to keep the Texas athletes in school.

Of course, that objective has many aspects. He must be a counselor, a guide, a taskmaster, a father confessor, a disciplinarian, a spur and, sometimes, a doggone unpopular fellow.

Contrary to some beliefs, the Brain Coach is definitely not a crutch. He's not something for athletes to lean on. He's there to keep a fire blazing under their bottoms and to keep them putting out an effort to stay in school and eligible for athletics.

The Guiding Hand

Many times when a raw youngster reports to a large university, he's completely confused. He doesn't know where to go, what to do, or whom to ask, and often he's too shy to find out. Just the confusion of establishing a steady routine is nervewracking to some youngsters.

The Brain Coach herds our freshmen athletes through the maze of registration and indoctrination with a careful and considerate hand. He takes them in a body on orientation tours and to indoctrination lectures. He sees that they are properly familiarized with the university before classes ever start. He helps with their registration and class schedules. (This is not only for football players, but all athletes.)

Four nights a week, the Brain Coach runs a supervised study hall from 7 until 9 o'clock. It is compulsory for all freshmen athletes.

Too often a boy has been told, "Just study *harder* and you'll do all right."

Hewlett says, "Study *smarter*," and he indicates the what, when, where, and how tools to be found on every campus. Tools that are so often overlooked by the beginning student.

While he does no tutoring himself, he has complete charge of our tutoring program. This program, by the way, costs us only one-third as much as before the Brain Coach days.

Goodwill Ambassador

And not the least of his values is Goodwill. The Brain Coach keeps a constant check on our athletes. He is the only person from the athletic department who contacts the professors or the administration. We don't have the basketball coach calling today, asking about this boy or that one. And the track coach calling the same prof tomorrow, asking about another youngster. Every coach works through the Brain Coach and this has created a wonderful relationship with the faculty. It has helped our interdepartmental relations in this phase more than you can imagine.

Mind you, never at any time does the Athletic Department ask any special favors from the faculty, other than just to keep us informed. The scholarship athlete is a working student who is earning his way through college. His athletic scholarship is an obligation to be aggressive in the classroom as well as on the field, the track, the court, and the diamond. This challenges most faculty members to supply helpful information about classroom progress, not only to keep athletes eligible but to help responsible students establish better study habits. The faculty recognizes this: to ask how an athlete is doing in his classes while there is still time to help him *earn* a passing grade is altogether different from approaching the faculty at the semester's *end* to see if something can be done about a failing average.

All we ask is, how is Joe getting along? Is he in trouble? Let us know and we'll strap a saddle on him. We've had professors call and report that a certain athlete is lagging in his class, that he got a low grade on his last test, and that he needs spurring up. The Brain Coach goes to work to find out why.

Master of All He Surveys

The Brain Coach has an office in the Athletic Department. He has a clear glass window fronting on the corridor so that he can see any athlete who passes by. He can spot them through the glass and have them inside his office for a talk in a matter of seconds.

The Brain Coach's office door has a slot cut into it. Every Monday, every athlete must fill out a "cut card," telling how many classes he failed to attend the previous week, and why, and drop it in the slot.

Frankly, the Brain Coach is not the most popular fellow among the younger athletes. But he's not running in a popularity contest. Naturally the people whom you must *make* study don't like to be pushed. But when they reach their senior year, then the Brain Coach is smothered with gratitude.

Survivor List

Very well then. The Brain Coach is a wonderful plan and sounds nice to the faculty and the parents, but what are the results? As I mentioned, there were only four seniors on the first squad we coached at Texas, back there in 1957.

In 1961, four years after the Brain Coach came into being, we had 10 seniors on our squad and all 10 were good ballplayers. Then we had an extra-point specialist who brought the senior total to 11.

In 1962, we had nine seniors of whom eight were first-stringers.

We'll gradually have more and we'll reach that level when we'll have 15 or 20 seniors playing on every squad. This, I believe, is vitally necessary for a winning operation. Almost any school will have certain years where there will be a large number of seniors. LSU, in 1962 for example, had 18 seniors. But you'd like to make it a practice to have that many *each* year. Make it a rule instead of an exception.

Since Lan Hewlett came to us, we have not lost a single upperclassman—to grades—whom we were depending on to help our football team. Had Hewlett not been on hand, we would have lost at least a dozen.

The athletes we've lost through "textbookitis" have mostly been in their freshmen year. That's when we don't know much about the youngsters. If they get by the first year and the Brain Coach gets his talons into their young hides, they are usually ours to have and to hold.

The Brain Coach travels with us, lives with us, enjoys the stimulating life of athletics. And you better believe it—we enjoy him! Every time we see a senior athlete perform; one who had a rocky going as a frosh or soph; we throw Lan another salute.

chapter fourteen

Public Relations

There was a time, I suppose, when a coach could jam a hunk of Brown Mule *into his jaw, climb into a greasy sweat-shirt, eschew a razor blade, bite off the heads of three sports-writers, chase at least one photographer up a tree, and concern himself solely with teaching football. This is no longer the case.*

Public relations has become just as important to a coach's career as the goal line defense. There is more press coverage, it is more wide-spread and more concentrated. Radio and television have added to the coach's exposure. Nowadays, the coach is constantly in the public eye.

The ability to deal with these added responsibilities is enviable. It's a phase of coaches' training that has been badly neglected in the past. Were I to advise a young man who knew he was going into coaching, I'd beg him to take college-level courses in public relations, public speaking, and—yes—maybe even journalism. And I can imagine howls from certain old-school sections of the audience. Even so, with a better sense of public relations, more coaches might enjoy steadier employment.

The Press

1. *Sportswriters.* Take the press. There is the old adage that a "closed mouth gathers no foot." Tell 'em nothing—just keep their glasses filled.

First, I don't see how a coach who is distrustful of sportswriters can possibly have good public relations.

Some coaches, doubtless, feel that the writers simply don't know enough to write intelligently about their par-

ticular teams. They suspect the writer doesn't understand enough technical football to report on the progress, or non-progress, of their heroes. Some are highly suspicious of writers, believing they are being led into a threatening valley of misquotes and controversial subjects.

You hear an occasional cry of "misquote" from a coach. This may well be. But it is indeed rare when an experienced, journeyman sports reporter will deliberately write the wrong words into his story.

Of course I do think (as Woody Hayes of Ohio State has often said) that there is a danger when inexperienced or non-professional reporters are given a set of quotes to play around with. Some of those lads are prone to embroider.

A couple years after we arrived at Texas, a reporter from the college paper asked about our team's prospects. I told him this should be the best team *we'd* had at Texas. The next day, the student paper had a headline: "*ROYAL SAYS TEAM BEST IN HISTORY.*"

This wasn't what I meant, of course. I meant the team should be the best we, as a staff, had coached at Texas.

And sometimes even a veteran writer can give an interpretation to an innocent quote that will change the entire meaning. *Example:* The season after James Saxton graduated, an experienced reporter asked me in a telephone conversation, "Do you miss Saxton?" I answered, "Yes," because any team would miss a breakaway runner like Saxton.

However, the story came out that Royal said, "We miss Saxton." Now there is a fine line between a true quote and a misconception. I didn't say those words; the writer asked them and I merely answered yes. Yet, when I was quoted as saying them, it sounded as if I were going around moaning, "We miss Saxton" as an alibi, which wasn't the truth.

But these instances are unusual and not worth worrying about. I've never felt any sportswriter who ever visited with me was planting questions to make me "look bad."

Perhaps I've been fortunate. I've heard of writers who took joy in slicing coaches to ribbons. Perhaps this could be partly the coaches' fault. Perhaps they're too suspicious of the writers, too evasive, or too reluctant to talk. A writer doesn't have to be overly sensitive to resent this distrust and interpret it as aloofness and unfriendliness.

2. ***Organized Conferences.*** Once a coach considers the pressboxers his friends, they'll be the first to defend him. Ninety percent of the writers will take up for a coach. At least, I've found them this way.

Coaches need writers. Writers need coaches. Without either, they'd both be in a jam.

Many schools use the "smoker" activity on the night before a Saturday game. The home college will rent a hotel suite or meeting room, provide refreshments and a place for local writers, visiting writers and the coaches of both schools to meet and have a big gabfest. These meetings, for some reason I've never determined, are called "smokers." But they're well worthwhile, for relaxation on the eve of a game, for visiting with old friends, for answering last minute questions about the coming game, and for public relations.

Several coaches—Wilkinson and Bryant among them—have a sort of open house after a game, for the staff and the attending writers. Sometimes this may be at the coach's home, more often at a hotel room or suite. Perhaps the room of one of the writers in town to cover the game. It gives everyone a chance to relax, replay the game or clear up any questions. Even more important, it may furnish the writers with material for follow-up stories on the game. We've done this at Texas, mainly on the recommendation of Jones Ramsey, our dedicated sports news director.

A couple hours after a home game, after the writers have wearily quit the pressbox and splashed water on their faces, they'll gather at some pre-determined meeting place. There'll be refreshments and snacks, whipped up by Jones, and usually Edith and I will drop by for a visit. Sometimes a coach doesn't feel too much like visiting after he's dropped a big one. But if you do it after the wins, you must do it after the losses.

The Alumni

1. *The Aggressive Type.* It was the late Herman Hickman, surveying his illustrious alumni at Yale, who gave this advice to his fellow coaches, out of the side of his mouth: "The secret is to keep the alumni sullen, but not mutinous."

Of course, the real secret is to keep the alumni, period.

I feel about alumni relations much as I do about press relations. You simply must have alumni support in order to organize and maintain a successful program.

There have been coaches who have bluntly told the alumni to stay out of their business; to keep out of their way. There âre some alumni to whom I've had to tell that. But these are rare exceptions.

Here again, there is no substitute for honesty. When we attend alumni meetings at various points over the state, we think it best to throw the program open to questions. The natural tendency for a coach, I suppose, is to shy away from alumni questions: the same old, "Well, coach, how're we gonna do Saturday?" business. However, part of the coaching duty is to *answer* these questions.

Now there is a difference in the way certain people can ask certain questions. There are some who will ask a question with the attitude of "I dare you to answer this." Of course a coach is not going to tolerate this. He resents it. But if a person, in all seriousness, wants to know something about our team because of a genuine interest, well, I don't mind his asking me why our pass defense is not better, or why we kick on third down so often.

I've had real good friends act apologetic when they'd ask something about our team, or word it in a delicate way, so I would not resent their questioning. In some cases, there is an area in which our team has failed and they want to know why. Yet they don't want me to interpret the question as a slight to the team or the coaching. These people, the ones who are genuinely interested in our fortunes, deserve and get every possible consideration. We honestly don't care how many questions we get, if they're sincere. And if we coaches can give them a good, honest, unevasive answer, it will help keep up their interest and, in turn, they will lend support to our athletic program.

2. ***The Inquisitive and Helpful.*** One day in Dallas, I had lunch with Col. D. Harold Byrd, a wealthy industrialist and supporter of university activities. He asked countless questions about our athletic program; detailed questions about our plans, and the whys and wherefores. Some people might have thought he was pretty darn nosey. Frankly, I was glad he was so interested and his questions were welcome. Out of that conversation came an idea that we'd kicked around for a couple years, about a Lettermen's Lounge to be built in the stadium. I mentioned this to the colonel in reviewing our long-range plans. He picked up the idea and ran with the ball right away. He started off the drive with a $10,000 donation and now we have an $80,000 room, beautifully furnished, a picture gallery, lounge area, soft drink bar, study area and recreational facilities. Our athletes use it during the school year, for study or relaxation or recreation. They may take dates there any night and dance as it is always chaperoned. The school's ex-lettermen gather there before a game and we have a catering service provide lunches. It's not unusual to have 500 former *Longhorns* visit the room on a single day.

This stadium show place is wonderful for the public relations side of the business. And it doesn't do the recruiting program a bit of harm either.

This is all a roundabout way of showing that the project never could have become a reality without the interest of Colonel Byrd and that luncheon hour spent answering a zillion questions.

3. ***The Die-Hards.*** Every school has its die-hards. We have a couple of exes from Dallas who dye their hair orange every football season. Texas has a Houston booster,

Jack Perry, who hasn't missed a *Longhorn* game in 15 years. He flies his own plane to the games. Even when the team had a 1-9 record, he still made every contest. "I was afraid we'd eventually win one and I wouldn't be there," he said. Another Houston friend of *Texas*, Johnny Holmes, has his private DC-3 painted and decorated in orange and white, with a big Longhorn painted on the tail.

4. *Awards to Contributors.* The Texas Athletic Department awards honorary letters to alumni who have made distinguished contributions to the program. At each road game, we invite three alumni to be guests of the squad for the day, sit on our bench during the game. One of the more enthusiastic backers, lawyer Bedford Wynne of Dallas, claimed he made a key substitution during Texas' *Cotton Bowl* victory over Mississippi.

I don't believe you can expect this support unless you keep the alumni informed. The evasive action should be reserved for the halfbacks. Woody Hayes says there are only two things a man is privileged to be biased about: his wife and his football team. After all, most alumni get a genuine kick out of following their school's athletic program, and the kidding and horseplay between alumni of other schools.

Texas' most hated rival is Texas A&M. And one of the *Aggies'* most renowned exes is Field Scovell, a Dallas insurance executive.

On New Year's Day, 1962, when Texas played Mississippi in the *Cotton Bowl,* Scovell went to the game with some friends, who happened to be Texas alumni. They were rawhiding him about being a turncoat, an *Aggie* who was supporting Texas in the *Cotton Bowl.*

Right in front of the main gate, Scovell stopped, reached in his pocket and pulled out a bar of soap and a washrag.

"I'm going to root for Texas today, all right," he said firmly, "but right after the game, I'm going to wash my mouth out with soap."

The Faculty

One phase of public relations that may sometimes be neglected is the relationship of the Athletic Department and the faculty.

The inclusion of our Brain Coach has helped greatly our faculty relationship at Texas. Once a week I go with Lan Hewlett to lunch at the Faculty Dining Room. I get a chance to speak to 50 or 75 professors and have lunch with a couple of them, just to form acquaintances.

And then, every home game, we invite three professors to be guests of the squad. Three different teachers from various departments of the university are invited by Lan. They join the squad on Saturday morning, eat with us, listen to the pre-game preparations, and then they sit on the bench with us during the game.

And what an eye-opener it is!

People sit up in the stands and see players several hundred feet away and they'll picture them as brutes who shave twice a day and eat nails for breakfast. But when these profs see some peach-fuzz kids sitting down to a pre-game meal, or carrying books under their arms the night before a game, they are amazed that these are the boys who are out there in that bulky armor playing on Saturday afternoon. We hope it gives the professors a new insight into the game and helps them to realize that the players are just students in one of the campus activities, no matter how much identity they lose when they climb inside that football equipment.

The Crank

At the University of Washington, I got my first experience with crank mail. I'll admit I didn't like it.

Frankly, I'm sort of a thin-skinned person and criticism bothers me. I found this to be true: the mail could be divided into a big stack of complimentary letters and four or five crank letters. Complimentary letters from good substantial alumni. And five letters from hecklers. And I'd go home at night and worry about those five crank letters, not even thinking about the complimentary mail.

At Washington, I would open a letter and look first for the signature. If the letter were signed (and many weren't), then I'd read it, give it some thought and consideration and answer it.

But when I moved to the University of Texas, I decided I had enough problems with the football project without trying to take on the cranks. So I very pointedly refused to read the uncomplimentary mail during the season.

My secretary, Blanche Rhodes, opens all the mail. If it is a crank letter or a complaining letter, she files it. I don't know who wrote me, or what they said. I tell myself I'll read the complaining mail during the off-season, but somehow I never get around to it. When the file gets full, I throw it away.

A Strange Bird: the Yellow Effigy-Hanger

And this brings me to another pet peeve of all coaches—the Effigy-Hangers. This effigy business has threatened to take over the country in the past few years. Almost any football coach can expect to find his model strung up on the nearest tree, bush or vine, sooner or later. This is the American Way of Life nowadays, like the filter cigarette and the disappearance of parking space.

You'll find the effigy, but you won't find any identification of the person who strung it up.

And most of the time you can read about it in the papers and hear it over the air: "*COACH JOE MCDOAKES HANGED IN EFFIGY.*"

And Coach Joe McDoakes and Mrs. Coach Joe Mc-

Doakes and all the little Coach Joe McDoakeses are shamed and wounded by some courageous citizen who strings up a dummy in the middle of the night, and then sneaks off to his lair, there to await the morning paper and the recognition given to his Deed of Valor.

The Effigy-Hanger is a rather sallow bird because of rare exposure to daylight. But he is well-nourished, he's kept sleek and glossy and good humored by the publicity he receives, and the needles he inflicts upon the coach and his family without exposing himself.

His sentiments, if honest, are his rightful property.

If he wishes to fire the coach, to intimate that he couldn't teach hop-scotch to Harvard graduates, to declare that the college would be much better off without Joe McDoakes—then let him hang old Joe in effigy. Let him string old Joe to the highest pole on Main Street.

But then, let him unfold a camp stool, park himself under the dummy and say to the passersby: "My name is Frederick Phan. I believe Ole Siwash should fire Joe McDoakes. I wish to intimate that Joe McDoakes could not teach hop-scotch to Harvard graduates. I declare Ole Siwash would be much better off without Joe McDoakes. This is my opinion, and you may quote me."

Then, let the reporter and the broadcaster take notes and dash to their typewriters or microphones. Everything is hunky-dory. The citizen has identified himself, expressed his thoughts loudly and clearly. This has something to do with the Bill of Rights.

But this is seldom the way it happens. There is neither honesty nor forthrightness involved. This is a smear hurled in the dead of night by an unidentified assailant. Take away the publicity given the effigy-hanger and he shrivels up. His plasma is cut off. He has no motive anymore; no justification; no fun.

Personally, I don't think news media should accord any more notice to the anonymous effigy-hanger than to the anonymous letter writer to its editorial page.

To express an opinion to a newspaper and see it in

print, a person writes a letter and signs his name. But the effigy-hanger, alas, doesn't have to identify himself to see his opinion in print. Several newspapers I know have stopped printing all stories with reference to effigies. Bravo.

The Bitter Brigade

Of course, there always will be some gripers among football followers. As the success of a team wanes, they multiply in shameful numbers. And as much as a coach may try to ignore his critics, leave his mail unread and the like, still the complaints seek him out in some weird osmosis.

1. *Yelps When We Win.* We've had seasons, winning seasons, in which some people objected to the way we won. When Texas employed constant use of the quick-kick, some critics said we had no confidence in our offense and were being non-aggressive.

I can remember one guy in Louisiana who was all torn up about Texas quick-kicking. He bombarded me with telegrams, saying that the team was "gutless" and was playing "give-up football."

Right before the A&M game one year, this fellow doubled his telegraphic efforts to scorn the quick-kick. I'll tell you how much effect this had on us. Just as fast as we got the wind, we rushed out of the huddle and quick-kicked and it won the game for us. His wires had a great effect.

This same fellow started sending wires to the Texas quarterback, Bobby Lackey, deploring the quick-kick. That's when a coach must step in. I took a personal interest in that, and called the fellow up. He did the crawdad act, as you would imagine.

It really burns me up when some of these cranks write a player who is just a student playing football, not for a living but for the love of the game, and who is trying to educate himself and prepare for a business or professional career. He should never be bothered by some pea-brained pest who has nothing better to do than make a world problem out of a football game.

I'm firmly convinced you're not going to please everybody, no matter what your record is, nor how high your national ranking. I was never more baffled about a season than the 1962 year. It was the roughest I've ever experienced.

It was the first unbeaten Texas team since 1923 and yet we received our share of criticism. There probably was never an undefeated team so maligned as this one. We were a defensive team, for one thing, and I've already reviewed the defensive logics in earlier chapters. And I suppose a defensive team will always be criticized.

Thank goodness, we were a defensive team in 1962! The Texas team scored 28 times that season, and the defense was responsible for 10 of those scores. Certainly that was the difference in a so-so season and a conference championship and a 10-game bib that had only one tie against it.

But this was a case of *how* you won, not *if* you won. It was rather ironic and I didn't mind speaking out about it. It hadn't been too many years ago that some Texas supporters were overjoyed over any sort of a victory. And here were some critics who were now questioning the manner in which we won.

We were winning with defense; that is, instead of the long-range offensive gains that Texas enjoyed the previous season.

I have discussed the 1961 season, the year of the Flip-Flop offense and the long dashes of James Saxton, and the tremendous upsurge in our offensive figures. That year was really an exception to our defensive way of thinking. It was against what we preach, but it worked. The following year, when Texas gained a 9-0-1 record and a No. 4 ranking in the national polls, was more typical of our thinking and coaching.

No one whose opinion I respected criticized us. But there were certain sneers and jokes at our conservative, defensive style of play.

2. ***Sneers When We Tie.*** For an example: The only smirch on the 1962 record was a 14-14 game with Rice.

The score stood at that reading with five minutes to

play in the game. Texas had the ball on its own 48-yard line, fourth down and one yard needed. We had a fine punter in sophomore Ernie Koy, who had delicate control of the ball. There was the distinct possibility that he might kick the ball out-of-bounds inside the Rice 10-yard line, or bounce it around so that we could kill the ball there. At worst, he would kick over the goal and Rice would have the ball on its own 20, with 80 yards of grass separating the *Owls* from winning points.

I have stressed repeatedly our staunch belief in *Field Position.* If Rice has the ball inside its own 20, I believe Texas is in a better position to score than Rice.

So we chose to punt on fourth down, rather than attempt to pick up the necessary yardage for a first down.

The punt was high and wonderfully covered. But, as fortune would have it, the ball came down and landed about on the Rice 20 and struck the heel of a Texas man, Perry McWilliams. Instead of bouncing forward, it took a backward jump like a wedge shot.

A Rice man scooped up the ball which had bounced backward over our coverage. It was fortunate that he didn't return it for a touchdown. By the time he was stopped, the *Owls* had the ball on their own 36 and, after a penalty against Texas, Rice had the favorable *Field Position* instead of us.

Texas was ranked No. 1 nationally at the time and our detractors jumped on that fact. They argued that we should have gambled on fourth down; that we had a national ranking to preserve; that the object of the game was to win, not to tie; and that Texas was forever playing in hopes the other team would fumble and not in hopes its own offense could score.

Of course, had we known that punt was going to strike a Texas foot and bounce backward, we would have gone for the fourth down rush. But we felt our chances of scoring were *better* by punting than anything else.

3. ***They Don't Understand Defense.*** Sometimes that

is a logic hard to explain. And that's one reason this book was written. (It's not hard to explain to coaches, but to the citizens in the stands and sometimes in the pressbox, some coaching decisions may seem overly conservative and downright cowardly.)

But this is the way it is, of course, when you have a defensive team. We believe that a team that plays well defensively will be more consistent than a team that plays well offensively. This is true in almost any sport you can name. And it takes more courage to play that type of game. As a coach, you know it's not so acceptable to fans. But the defensive game is the game that wins. People may like an offensive team, but they like a winner more.

As for the argument that we should have run on that fourth down play because we had a No. 1 national ranking to protect, well, that's rather shallow logic. To begin with, our scoring chances were *better* by punting. And even if they weren't, our goal is to win conference championships. We could have won our Southwest Conference title (and did) with a tie. Any No. 1 ranking is a mythical thing and a flimsy platform. A conference championship is a tangible accomplishment. You must play for such accomplishments, and let the national business take care of itself.

Pressure Cooker

There was a funny aftermath to that 14-14 tie with Rice, the one that had brought some sneers in our direction. A couple weeks later, we played Baylor, a wide-open passing team.

Baylor defensed us for the run and almost ignored the passing threat. Texas had a great day in the air. Tommy Wade, heretofore our third quarterback, was inserted as the starting signal-caller and he hit on 11 passes, and the *Longhorn* offense had a splendid day indeed. There were those who thought we had opened up the Texas offense, had started throwing the ball more, because of the criticism.

Figure 16: In the 1962 Texas-Baylor game, Jim Hudson (22) waits confidently for one of Tom Wade's 11 completed passes. Strategy helped to win this game as Texas went to the air to counter Baylor's strong preparations for an expected ground attack.

I was asked, "Well, Coach, aren't you happy that you were able to shut up some of that criticism about the Texas offense?"

I was happy that we won the game and for that reason only. We were playing Baylor and not the critics.

As for criticism making us change our offense, that also got a negative answer. Our coaching staff plans an attack that we feel is best suited to winning a given ball game. I hope we never get into a position where we'll be weak enough to give in to criticism over our better judgment. Also I hope I'm never stubborn or bull-headed enough to reach the position of refusing to change, simply because someone else suggested it.

A coach must follow what he believes in. Abraham Lincoln put it this way:

> I do the very best I can, the best I know how, and will continue to do so until the end. If the end proves me to be right, nothing else matters. And if, in the end, I am wrong, ten angels swearing that I was right will not make it so.

The best thing a coach can hope for is to please the majority. And the only way to please the majority is to win.

Index

H

I

J

K

L

M

Q

R

S

T

W

Y

Z